BOOKS BY JAMES D. HORAN

WORLD WAR II

Action Tonight: The story of the Destroyer O'Bannon

WESTERN FRONTIER

Desperate Men
Desperate Women
Pictorial History of the Wild West (with Paul Sann)
Across the Cimarron
The Great American West
The Wild Bunch

CIVIL WAR

Mathew Brady: Historian With a Camera
Confederate Agent
C.S.S. Shenandoah: The Memoirs of Lieutenant Commanding James I. Waddell

NOVELS

King's Rebel
Seek Out and Destroy
The Shadow Catcher
The Seat of Power

CRIME

The Pinkerton Story (with Howard Swiggett)
The D.A.'s Man
The Mob's Man

CONTEMPORARY HISTORY

The Desperate Years: A Pictorial History of the Thirties

AMERICAN PHOTOGRAPHERS SERIES

Timothy O'Sullivan: America's Forgotten Photographer

TIMOTHY O'SULLIVAN:
AMERICA'S FORGOTTEN PHOTOGRAPHER

TIMOTHY O'SULLIVAN

AMERICA'S FORGOTTEN PHOTOGRAPHER

THE LIFE AND WORK OF THE BRILLIANT PHOTOGRAPHER WHOSE CAMERA RECORDED THE AMERICAN SCENE FROM THE BATTLEFIELDS OF THE CIVIL WAR TO THE FRONTIERS OF THE WEST

BY JAMES D. HORAN

BONANZA BOOKS • NEW YORK

PHOTO CREDITS

Eastman House: pages x, 6, 7 (upper left), 9, 17, 26, 222–23, 224 (bottom), 225 (bottom), 229, 233–35, 310

James D. Horan Civil War and Western Americana Collection: pages 30, 40, 93 (lower right), 105 (bottom), 115 (top), 130 (bottom), 152 (top), 154, 158–59, 162, 164, 167, 169, 171, 175–85, 187–92, 194, 198–205, 206 (top), 216, 218, 219 (right), 239–40, 246, 254, 263–65, 269, 271, 273–75, 281 (bottom), 284–87, 288 (top, lower left), 290, 293–96, 300–4, 309

G. T. Howe, M.D., Rochester, New York: page 25 (right)

Library of Congress: pages 2, 3, 12 (top, lower left), 13, 16, 28, 32 (top, lower right), 35, 37, 39, 42–58, 60–65, 66 (top), 67, 68 (top), 70 (lower left), 71, 73 (top left), 74, 75 (bottom), 76–88, 90, 92 (top), 94 (top, bottom left), 95–97, 98 (bottom), 100–4, 105 (top), 106–8, 110–13, 114 (bottom), 116–17, 118 (bottom), 119–21, 122 (top), 124 (top), 125 (top), 126 (top), 129 (top), 130 (top), 131–32, 134 (bottom), 136, 138, 139 (top), 140–44, 145 (top), 146 (bottom), 147, 149

Museum of the City of New York: page 15

National Archives: pages 33, 59 (top), 66 (bottom), 146 (top), 170, 186, 193, 195–97, 206 (bottom), 208–9, 213, 217, 219 (left), 220 (lower right), 224 (bottom), 225 (top), 226–28, 230–32, 242–43, 247–48, 251, 253, 255–56, 259–62, 266–67, 270, 272, 276–80, 281 (top), 282–83, 288 (lower right), 291–92, 306–7, 318

New York County Clerk's Office: pages 10, 14, 20 (lower right)

New York Historical Society: pages 4, 18–19, 20 (top left), 21, 23–24, 25 (left), 41, 58 (bottom), 68 (lower left and right), 69, 70 (top, lower right), 72, 75 (top), 91, 93 (lower left), 94 (lower right), 98 (top), 109, 114 (top), 115 (bottom), 118 (top), 122 (bottom), 123, 124 (bottom), 126 (bottom), 127, 128 (top), 129 (bottom), 133, 134 (top), 135, 137, 139 (bottom), 145 (bottom), 148, 152 (bottom), 160–61, 210, 212, 220 (top, lower left), 250, 268, 297–99, 305, 308, 311

New York Public Library: pages 8, 11, 12 (lower right), 36

Lloyd Ostendorf: page 128 (bottom)

Staten Island Historical Society: pages 20 (top right), 22

Library of Congress Catalog Card Number 66-20922

Printed in the United States of America

This edition published by Bonanza Books,
a division of Crown Publishers, Inc.,
by arrangement with Doubleday & Company, Inc.

a b c d e f g h

For Jimmy, the Horan Cameraman

CONTENTS

The only known photograph of Tim O'Sullivan, taken in 1870 while on the Darién Expedition, captioned, "Photographer at Pinog

AN AUTHOR'S REPORT ON HIS SEARCH INTO THE LIFE OF TIMOTHY H. O'SULLIVAN

One of the most daring yet sensitive of the Civil War and Western frontier photographers was Timothy H. O'Sullivan, whose camera and glass plates captured the American scene from the misty fields of Gettysburg to the roaring gold camp that was Virginia City. He served under many generals, saw action on many fronts both land and sea, brought his camera to the jungles of Darién (Panama), then to the deserts of the early southwest and the mountain ranges of the One Hundredth Meridian. Ironically, many of his great Civil War photographs have at times been erroneously credited to Mathew B. Brady, his friend and his mentor.

I first became acquainted with O'Sullivan's works more than a decade ago when I was doing research for my biography of Brady. In the beginning he was only a name, sometimes "T. O'Sullivan," etched on the edge of a glass plate, or simply a credit line under his photographs in the *Photographic Sketch Book of the War,* published by Alexander Gardner in 1865. Fortunately Gardner, unlike Brady, felt that each photographer should have credit for the work he did.

The extent of O'Sullivan's work can be determined by an examination of the Gardner *Sketch Book.* Over half the negatives were made by O'Sullivan. They are sensitive, poignant photographs of cannon-shattered homes, proud officers, winding trenches and bleak huts, homey scenes of camp life and his unforgettable "Harvest of Death" at Gettysburg. We can recall the stirring dramas, the soaring words about this greatest of American battles, but the misty morning, the far-off man on horseback, the bloated, plundered dead, are real, not imagined. The day before, these men were alive; they had charged across this field under taut banners, before they fell. This is how they looked in death.

His frontier photographs are the same; O'Sullivan's Apaches leaning on their Winchesters to stare into the lens nearly a century ago are still menacing.

After I had finished my Brady biography I set out to do one on O'Sullivan and to authenticate as many of his photographs as I could. I had experienced a great deal of difficulty gathering material on Brady's life but O'Sullivan presented a far more difficult task.

There were few clues, only his name, a four-line obituary in the photographic trade magazine and some plates. For more than ten years I searched for details, wrote hundreds of letters, and examined countless yellowing court records, death, birth, and marriage notices in an effort to find out something about Timothy H. O'Sullivan the man.

Gradually the minutiae began to collect and the life of O'Sullivan took form. A self-portrait taken in 1870 when he was a member of Commander Selfridge's Darién (Panama) Expedition shows him to be a lean, tough, mustachioed young man with a sun-darkened face, standing beside his huge camera in the native village. By this time he was undoubtedly one of the most experienced expeditionary photographers in the country.

The memoirs and the diaries of men with whom he shared hardships in the deserts and mountains of the West show he was a modest, lighthearted companion who never hesitated to risk his life for the company. His commanders discovered that he was a born leader of men and more than once he was given command of side and forage parties traveling through dangerous Indian country.

His obituary stated he died in Staten Island; months of searching court records in that community finally helped me to put together a number of facts of his early life on that beautiful island. In Albany a tedious search among the dead records of the New York Department of Health at last unearthed his death certificate with its vital statistics. Old land maps, census records, and even the account book of a long-dead undertaker helped in the struggle to find anything about O'Sullivan. The bare mention of the photographer's name on a bill or receipt became a singular victory.

The search for his photographs was easier; others who had been impressed with the young Irishman's work had helped to blaze a trail. One great difficulty in establishing credit for Civil War photographs was the habit of Brady—and others—of attaching their names to every photograph that passed through their hands.

O'Sullivan served his apprenticeship with Brady but left the old photographer to join Alexander Gardner, that intellectual Scot, when Gardner and Brady parted shortly after the start of the Civil War.

It was quite obvious to me after I had combed through the Brady-Handy Collection in 1954, then restricted in the Library of Congress, that Brady had been more a manager than a photographer, particularly during the Civil War. Yet Brady deserves fame as the man who originated and who sustained, as far as he could, a continuing enterprise for preserving the negatives he and his men made of the Civil War, adding to this collection just about anything he could lay his hands on.

There is little doubt that Brady was anything but ethical when it came to giving credit. But this can be understood when we see Brady not as a photographer but as the head of a photographic business, such as Associated Press. (As a former editor of a metropolitan daily I examined countless pictures every day from the world's leading wire service and seldom found credit given to an individual photographer.)

Undoubtedly Brady, a superb portrait photographer, made many of the portraits of the Civil War figures (Lee after the surrender), but his weak eyes and his reluctance because of the cost and his responsibilities, kept him from following the armies. A check of his own catalogue published in 1869 reveals that half the battlefield pictures were made in Virginia within traveling distance by his photographic wagon from Washington. It was O'Sullivan, the Gardners, Alexander and James; John Reekie, James F. Gibson, George M. Barnard who followed the armies, shared their hardships, and made the large part of the extraordinary photographic history of the Civil War.

When O'Sullivan brought his camera to the Civil War battlefields and the Western frontier of the 1860s and 1870s, the collodion wet-plate process could not cope with movement. On the battlefields O'Sullivan must have had an enormous task caring for his cumbersome equipment and keeping up with the movement of the armies, advancing or retreating. While the Civil War camera was best at recording material, horses, wagons, ships, officers and men, O'Sullivan managed to record batteries under fire or exchanging fire, railroads and bridges destroyed by Jackson's foot cavalry.

If at any time the war moved too quickly and the Union troops were swept up in a retreat before O'Sullivan had a chance to take his photographs, either he or some other photographer would wait and come back that way again. For example, we find photographs taken of Mechanicsville in April 1865, although the battle was fought there in July 1862. At Mechanicsville in

April, General Fitz-John Porter fiercely fought Stonewall Jackson's men to a standstill but his troops were ordered withdrawn during the night. James F. Gibson, Brady's photographer and later partner, could not photograph the battle of Mechanicsville; it had to wait until John Reekie, who worked with O'Sullivan under Alexander Gardner, passed that way nearly three years later.

O'Sullivan's photographic work of the Western frontier in the 1860s and 1870s is unsurpassed; William H. Jackson is better known but O'Sullivan was there before him and his photographs in my opinion are as good if not better.

There are several valleys, mountains, and rivers named after Western photographers but O'Sullivan, one of the greatest, has no living monument to his work. I hope that some snow-capped peak, quiet stream, or lonely valley will someday carry the name of Timothy H. O'Sullivan in tribute to this gallant American photographer.

O'Sullivan's photographs are in the National Archives, Library of Congress, United States Geological Survey, New York Historical Society, Art Institute of Chicago, the George Eastman House, Rochester, and the New York Public Library's Rare Book Room. Some of his original glass plates are in the National Archives, along with at least two grooved boxes he may have used to store plates while on the Wheeler Expedition. A beautiful copy of Gardner's *Sketch Book of the Civil War* is in the New York Historical Society.

To put together the bare bones of O'Sullivan's life and flesh it out, required the help and assistance of many people and it is a pleasure to acknowledge their kindness and contributions.

Heading the list must be Mrs. Hermine Baumhofer, of Dayton, Ohio, who located O'Sullivan's sole letter and letters of recommendation when he was seeking the appointment as photographer for the Treasury Department in 1880. Miss Josephine Cobb, Specialist in Iconography, National Archives, undoubtedly one of our top experts on Civil War photography and photographers, was a tremendous help. No book on the subject can be written without her assistance. Mr. Arthur B. Carlson, Curator of the Maps and Prints Division and the Randauer Collection of the New York Historical Society was of enormous assistance in helping me locate and select O'Sullivan's stereoscopic views of the Civil War and of the Wheeler Expedition. His advice and encouragement on those wonderful Monday afternoons were great contributions to this book. As always the Society's excellent research library was invaluable along with the aid and advice of an old friend, Mr. James Heslin, Director, Miss Shirley Beresford, Reference Librarian, and that expert without peer on the Civil War and Western frontier, Mr. Sylvester Vigilante.

I owe a special note of thanks to Mr. Frank Forrester, Information Officer, United States Department of Interior, Geological Survey, and Mrs. Aleta Leiber, of the department's Non-technical Unit, who found the field notes of G. K. Gilbert relating to O'Sullivan and the Wheeler ascent of the Colorado and who also located some interesting O'Sullivan photographs in the Denver office.

In the Denver headquarters of the U. S. Geological Survey, there are five of O'Sullivan's Western photographs which are not listed in either the Archives or Library of Congress files.

Once again Mr. Karl Pretshold and his staff of the New York City Department of Health and Mr. Clark LeBoeuf, Director, Office of Vital Records (Department of Health), Albany, helped me to reconstruct the life of a great American through their files and records; while Mr. George Feinstein, clerk in charge of the Division of Records, County Clerk's Office, New York County, and Mr. James Fitzgerald assisted me in documenting the legend that Brady and O'Sullivan lived on Staten Island.

I owe a special note of thanks to Mr. Raymond Fingado of the Staten Island Historical Society, who searched long and hard for glass plates, clippings, city maps and charts to help me reconstruct the life and times of Timothy O'Sullivan. Gail K. Schneider of the Staten Island Institute of Arts and Sciences was particularly helpful in researching old records and contemporary articles on Brady's Grymes Hill home.

Mr. Beaumont Newhall, Director of the George Eastman House, Rochester, and Robert Bretz, Assistant Curator, Collections, were particularly helpful in locating and copying O'Sullivan's photographs of the Darién Expedition.

Mr. Hirst D. Milhollen, Specialist in Photography, Library of Congress, Mr. Milton Kaplan, and Miss Virginia Daiker again were helpful with suggestions and the listing of O'Sullivan photographs in the Library of Congress.

The entire staff of the Still Picture section of the National Archives was extremely cooperative, courteous, and helpful, and as always Mr. Joe Thomas was on hand with expert advice, suggestions, and good humor.

Mr. John Barr Tompkins, Head, Public Services, of the Bancroft Library, University of California, Berkeley, located for me the extremely interesting and little-known frontier newspaper clippings which described O'Sullivan's experiences in Death Valley with the two guides; and Mr. Elbert L. Huber, Chief, Navy and Military Service Branch, National Archives, found the log of the U.S.S. *Guard,* the storeship to which O'Sullivan was assigned during the Darién Expedition. Mr. Richard A. Bartlett, Associate Professor of History at the Florida State University, author of *Great Surveys of the American West,* one of the best I've read on the subject, took time from a busy schedule to tell me what he had found on O'Sullivan during his long and extensive research.

Of all the notes of thanks, however, the strongest should be to my wife, Gertrude, who never stopped insisting that I do the book—and then finish it—and under tremendous deadline pressure, corrected and typed the manuscript.

Horan's Boondocks

TIMOTHY O'SULLIVAN:
AMERICA'S FORGOTTEN PHOTOGRAPHER

1

A SHY MAN

It was a quiet, beautiful Pennsylvania valley. In its center was a small village of farms and white clapboard houses. There were dusty roads leading in and out of the town: Carlisle Road, Harrisburg Road, and Mummasburg Road which crossed wooded Oak Hill. On Seminary Ridge, about half a mile west of the village was the Lutheran Theological Seminary which gave the ridge its name. Directly south was Cemetery Ridge. Three miles from the village Cemetery Ridge ended in a series of rocky ridges with a peak the natives called Round Top. North of it was Little Round Top. Five hundred yards west was an eerie place of thick underbrush and large boulders, hurled about, it seemed, as if by a frenzied giant.

"Fashioned by the Devil's own hand," they said.

The village was called Gettysburg and on that July day it was one of the saddest battlefields in American history. Thousands of uncovered dead, blue and gray, covered the fields and ridges. Men lay near overturned guns or where they fell in the tasseled wheat fields.

It had been raining that morning, not with the sudden violence of summer but rather the thin, ugly drizzle of November. The barrels of the smashed cannons glistened and so did the flanks of the horses. The uniforms of the dead were sodden.[1]

The burial parties had been working since sunup. There were so many dead men to bury there wasn't time to dig the graves very deep and some of the dead weren't even wrapped in blankets or tent rolls. There wasn't a sound, only the clink of spades as they hit a stone or the measured slam as a wooden slab was made firm in the wet dirt.

Nobody paid much attention to the wagon that drove up with two men in it. It was much like a carriage but covered on all sides by black cloth or canvas. The man driving was not a soldier. He was slender, in his twenties and when he jumped down he was carrying a camera. The other man was shorter, no more than five feet seven, with a sharply pointed goatee. He seemed troubled with weak eyes and peered through thick glasses. He wore a queer, flat straw hat, a linen duster, and was obviously older than the driver.

They walked about the battlefield: Missionary Ridge, the stone wall where Pickett charged, the wide field where the dead of the 24th Michigan Infantry—the Iron Brigade—stretched almost to the far fence, the point under the large dripping tree on the peak of Round Top where the Union guns had caught a small group of Confederates. Once the younger man took his camera into Devil's Den, where the thick underbrush was now ripped by the violence of the battle, to

O'Sullivan's view of Brady in the wheat field, scene of General McPherson's death at Gettysburg.

silently photograph the stiffened bodies. Then to the peak of the ridge where the solitary Rebel sharpshooter lay sprawled, face to the sky, his rifle near his head. There was also Lossers Barn with the smashed fence and the dead horses and men of the 9th Massachusetts Battery. Finally the pasture field on the Confederate right where the dead lay in rows and the wheat field where General Reynolds fell. Here the older man walked into the field with another man, probably a local resident who pointed to the spot where Reynolds died. As he pointed, the younger man snapped the picture.

In New York a few weeks later a large part of *Harper's Weekly* was devoted to the woodcuts based on pictures the young photographer had taken. They were also reproduced in large numbers and widely circulated to bring to Americans at home the grim meaning of war. The photographs stirred the country and Oliver Wendell Holmes saw them and wept.

As usual the woodcuts based on the photographs had the credit line, "Photo by Brady."[2]

This was the way it always was in New York; Mathew B. Brady was the most talked-about photographer. He knew and was friendly with statesmen, generals, kings and queens. He insisted many times that his picture of Lincoln before the Cooper Institute address had helped to make him President. But there were some who said he was trying to create a legend. When he set out to photograph the Civil War he insisted that photographs he distributed had to be labeled, "Photo by Brady" no matter who had actually operated the camera.

If the young photographer at Gettysburg felt that this was an injustice he never publicly or privately said so, for Timothy H. O'Sullivan was a shy man, perhaps even a lonely man who never sought praise or credit. He seemed content to let his magnificent photographs speak for themselves.[3]

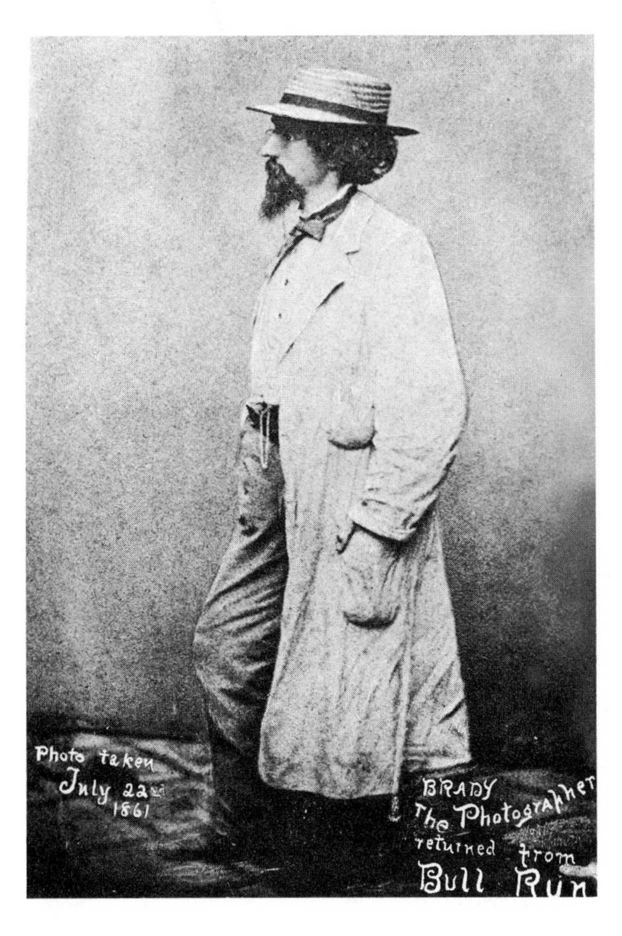

Mathew B. Brady after the First Battle of Bull Run. Brady insisted that his assistants take his picture for history when he returned to Washington with the first plates of the war. Photographer unknown.

Gettysburg was not the only battlefield O'Sullivan knew. He lugged his cumbersome camera and equipment from Second Manassas to McLean's immortal clapboard house at Appomattox. He followed the Army of the Potomac, bouncing along the rutted roads in his traveling studio, setting his negatives in the canvas darkroom that reeked of chemicals. Twice his camera was knocked from his hand by shell fragments but he always got his pictures.[4]

He took countless glass plates, many of them more revealing, more laden with character and the simple brutal horror of war, than some of the polished prints produced by the modern camera of World War II. There are the tired, bone-weary Union veterans, the arrogant political generals and their insufferable aides; the gunners ready to "fan the vent"; the long lines of wagons and horses—one can almost hear the creaking wheels and the labored hoofbeats on the planked roadbeds of the pontoon bridges. But he also caught the personal, the human side of the Civil War; the proud hand in the coat, the beards, mustaches, sideburns of every variety, the jackboots and carelessly unbuttoned collars and ankle-long coats—all that can tell Americans a century later of their war and the character of the people who fought it.

But the marvelous thing about O'Sullivan is that unlike Brady he never stopped photographing history-making events after the war had ended. Legend claims he turned down Brady's offer of the job of managing the Washington studio after Appomattox.

This seems to fit in with his character. While he appears to have been a shy, reserved man, he also seemed restless, disdainful of ledgers, desks, appointments, and the stuffy, florid galleries of the East. After the war he seemed eager to be in the company of those strange, indomitable men who, lured by the unknown, surveyed the vast regions of this wide land, always seeking what lay beyond the next hill.

From the late sixties to the mid-seventies O'Sullivan lugged his 20 by 24 camera from Death Valley to Virginia City as official photographer for the government geographical surveys. He suffered incredible hardships yet took many magnificent pictures of that stirring Western land to change it from myth to reality. When there were no government expeditions to the West he brought his camera to the jungle as official photographer for the naval party that cut its way through the Isthmus of Darién (Panama).[5]

When O'Sullivan was making his impressive photographs, the most advanced photographic process was the wet-plate technique. The photographer had to make his own wet plate in the field immediately before exposure, then develop it after exposure without delay. As these operations had to be made in a subdued orange-red light a portable darkroom had to be handy. O'Sullivan on most of his Western trips used a Civil War type ambulance, drawn by two to

One of Brady's What-Is-It Wagons, portable darkrooms used in photographing the Civil War. O'Sullivan used a similar type. Photographer unknown.

four mules. When he had to abandon the wagon and use only pack mules to cross the mountain passes, he carried a small pyramidal tent with orange calico which opened up and could be set up on a tripod.

After coating the clear glass plate with the sticky collodion, he rushed it outside, took his picture and brought it back to either the ambulance-darkroom or the tiny tent, to fix, wash, and develop. For each exposure there were six separate operations. As W. H. Jackson wrote Robert Taft, author of *Photography and the American Scene:*

"When hard pressed for time I had to make a negative in fifteen minutes from the time the first rope was thrown from the pack to the final repacking."

But the exposure and developing of his plates was only one of the incredible problems O'Sullivan faced. He had to push, carry, haul—by mule or on his own back—his giant camera across the wildest country in the United States and later in the jungles of Darién. There were times when he undoubtedly returned empty-handed and we have a hint of what he went through from what Frederick S. Dellenbaugh, a member of the second Powell Expedition, wrote in his journal:

"Clem and Bonnemort arrived from an expedition to make photographs down the Kanab Canyon . . . they had met with bad luck and did not get a single negative. The silver bath got out of order and the horse carrying the camera fell off a cliff and fell on a camera, which had been tied on the outside of the pack, with a result that need not be described . . ."

We don't have the exact amount of supplies O'Sullivan carried up and down the valleys and across the mountains and wild rivers of America in the 1860s and 1870s but if the amount carried by his contemporary W. H. Jackson is any criterion, O'Sullivan must have included: stereoscopic camera with one or more pairs of lens; 5 by 8 camera box plus lens; dark tent; tripods; 10 pounds of collodion; 36 ounces of silver nitrate; 2 quarts of alcohol; 10 pounds iron sulphate; packages of filters; 1¼ pounds potassium cyanide; 3 yards Canton flannel; 1 box Rottenstone; 3 negative boxes; 6 ounces nitric aid; 1 quart varnish; developing and fixing trays; dozen and a half bottles of various sizes; glass for negatives, 400 pieces.

One can only shudder at the mental picture of O'Sullivan shepherding this fragile, cumbersome but vital load on the backs of his "cantankerous" mules as he and the rest of the King Expedition inched their way across the creaking surface of the snow-topped mountains in the bone-numbing moonlight . . .

O'Sullivan gained a stern technical training in the Civil War which resulted in priceless historic photographs of that conflict, but the hardships he endured on those battlefields and in the mountains and deserts of the Western frontier obviously wore down his lean and lanky frame. He must have felt the first symptoms of tuberculosis when he returned from the last Wheeler Expedition in 1875. Only a few years later he was desperately seeking an appointment as photographer for the Treasury Department and his many famous friends rallied to help him. But he held it only for a few months before returning to his father's home in Staten Island to die at the age of forty-two.

It is heart-rending to discover that not even the local weekly thought he deserved an obituary. He only rated four lines in a trade journal.

He sleeps today in an obscure grave in an ancient Staten Island cemetery, unknown, unhonored, and unsung.[6]

This book is his tribute.

2

THE EARLY YEARS

It was a hot and sticky day in August 1839 when Louis Jacques Mande Daguerre, citizen of France, sat fidgeting in the French Academy of Sciences. He was listening impatiently as François Arago, a great savant of his day, read to the assembled men of wisdom a description of the process with which Daguerre had just astonished the world of science.

The French government had agreed to grant Daguerre an annual income of six thousand francs as compensation for revealing to the world the magic process by which he had produced pictures on the face of a copper plate.

In that hushed and hot room, photography, born in the ingenious mind of Louis Jacques Mande Daguerre, had made its world debut.

In Paris at the time when Arago was carefully reading his speech about copper plates, iodine vapor, camera obscura, and such, was Samuel F. B. Morse, inventor of the electromagnetic telegraph. Morse was fascinated with Daguerre's invention and ordered a Daguerreotype camera built to his own specifications. He carefully followed Arago's description of Daguerre's technique which was not too complicated . . .

A sheet of copper was coated with silver, well polished and cleaned. The surface was exposed in a small box to iodine vapors at ordinary temperature until the silvered side turned a golden yellow color. The time required was anywhere from five to thirty seconds. The sensitized plate was then placed into the camera, five to ten minutes in the summer and from ten to twelve minutes in the winter. The negative was developed by being exposed in a closed box to mercury vapors heated to 167° Fahrenheit. The

Louis Jacques Mande Daguerre, who gave the Daguerreotype its name. Joseph Nicéphore Niepce was one of the inventors of photography but it was Daguerre who popularized it. This Daguerreotype was taken by Jean Baptiste Sabatier-Blot in 1844.

Samuel F. B. Morse, inventor of the telegraph, and first American to learn the Daguerreotype process from Daguerre himself in Paris. Morse took the first Daguerreotype portrait in the world on September 20, 1839, of his wife and daughter who sat on the roof of a building from ten to twenty minutes "in full sunlight and with their eyes closed." Brady learned the Daguerreotype process from Morse either by the inventor's public lectures or in private classes.

plate was then washed with hyposulphite of soda.

Some time in March 1839 Morse saw the Daguerreotypes and wrote about them in a letter to the New York *Observer:*

"They are produced on a metallic surface, the principal pieces about 7 inches by 5, and they resemble aquatint engravings; for they are in simple chiaro oscuro, and not in colors, but the exquisite minuteness of the delineation cannot be conceived. No painting or engraving ever approached it. For example: In a view up the street, the distant sign would be perceived, and the eye could just discern that there were lines of letters upon it, but so minute as not to be read with the naked eye. By the assistance of a

Rare picture of the camera of Alexander Wolcott, a New York pioneer photographer, built the year after photography was born. Wolcott was issued the first patent in the United States for photography. He also opened the world's first portrait studio in New York on March 4, 1840.

powerful lens which magnified fifty times, applied to the delineation, every letter was clearly and distinctly legible, and so also were the minutest breaks and lines in the walls of the buildings; and the pavements of the streets. The effect of the lens upon the picture was in a great degree like that of the telescope in nature . . . The impressions of interior views are Rembrandt perfected."

Anyone who saw Daguerre's works were impressed; nothing like this had been seen before. Experiments had been made, but no one had been able to fix an image of the camera. Morse knew the frustrations, for years before he had made numerous experiments with the camera obscura.

In August, Daguerre's manual giving instructions in how to take Daguerreotypes, appeared in Paris. It was a pamphlet giving detailed instructions how to construct a camera. Before the year ended it had been translated into many languages. Morse, like many others, undoubtedly learned the elements of photography from this pamphlet.

Morse and his newly constituted camera arrived in the United States that fall. In October he exhibited a view of the Unitarian Church, taken from the third floor of New York University, with an exposure of fifteen minutes.

Stories were now being printed announcing to the world the process of photography. The New York *Morning Herald* was able to tell its readers how one of its reporters had paid a visit to Chilton's on Broadway to see the first public display of the Daguerreotype. The scene on display "embraced" St. Paul's Church on the corner of Fulton and Broadway and a part of the Astor House, then on the corner of what is now Vesey Street and Broadway.

"All this," the *Herald*'s story said, "was on a copper plate equal in size to a miniature painting."[7]

Included in the story was the process, Daguerre's method of producing pictures on copper plates. Pretty ladies with "small feet" were urged to have their likeness taken, and in a grand manner the reporter ended his story with telling his readers that this new art "looks like a fairy."

And then on the scene emerged Mathew B. Brady, the man who would bring O'Sullivan into the world of photography and instruct him in all that he knew.

Brady's birthplace is still uncertain. Francis Trevelyan Miller, the editor of the monumental *Photographic History of the Civil War* put Brady's birthplace as Cork, Ireland, but Brady told Gath Townsend, the former *World* war correspondent, he was born in Warren County in upper New York State "about 1823–24." His death certificate shows that his parents, Andrew and Julia, were born in the United States.[8]

He left his frontier home in his teens and traveled to Saratoga where he met William Page, destined to become a well-known American artist. C. Edwards Lester, the art critic, later claimed that Page encouraged Brady to sketch "giving him a bundle of crayons."

Brady and Page came to New York city in about 1840, just when O'Sullivan was born. Page opened a studio on Chambers Street. It can be assumed that they also shared quarters in this mushrooming city, then in the last grip of a national financial panic. It is said that Brady found a job as a clerk in A. T. Stewart's store then located on Chambers and Broadway.

Probably the earliest portrait of Mathew B. Brady, made about 1845, less than two years after he had opened his Broadway studio. This lithograph accompanied an article on Brady and his work written by C. Edwards Lester, leading art critic of his day in the first issue of the Photographic Art Journal, *January 1851. The lithograph was made by F. D'Avignon, whose name is in the left corner.*

Three years later, 1843, the New York City directory listed him as a jewel case manufacturer. In the spring of that year Brady wrote to Albert Sands Southworth, probably one of the most famous of pioneer Daguerreotypists, soliciting business for his new line of miniature cases.

He wrote:

"I have been engaged for some time past in manufacturing (sic) miniature cases for some of the principal operators in this city and recently in business for myself and anxious for encouragement. I have got up a new style case with embossed top and extra fine diaframe (sic). This style of case has been admired by all the principal artists in the city. If you feel desirous to see my style of case if you favor me with an answer

New York June 17 1843

Mr Southworth

Sir I Beg Leave of Communicating these few lines soliciting your attention I Being informed by S & P Champney and several of your friends that you are one of the most successful Prof of Daguerreotype and doing the most extensive business in boston and invariably use a great number of Miniature Cases i have been engaged some time past in Manufacturing Miniature cases for some of the principal operators in this City and Recently business for myself and anxious for encouragement. i have got up a new style Case with embossed top and extra fine [illegible] frame this style of Case has been admired by all the principal artists in the City if you feel Desirous to see my style of Cases if you Will favor me with an answer I will Will send them by Harnden Express if my style of cases should suit you I can supply you on Reasonable terms.

Yours. M B Brady

162 Fulton near Broadway opposite St Pauls Church

Mathew B. Brady's letter to Southworth, a rare sample of Brady's handwriting.

I will send them by Horse Express. If my style of case should suit you I can supply them on reasonable terms."[9]

While there is no evidence that Southworth ordered any of Brady's new style cases, the ambitious young artist decided to establish himself as a photographer.

Brady was either taught Daguerreotype privately by Samuel F. B. Morse or attended his public lectures as did many of the early New York photographers.

Some time in 1844 young Brady, then about twenty-one, felt that he had learned all that Morse could teach him and with the small cash capital he had saved, opened his first gallery.

It was in the heart of the Times Square of his time—Fulton Street and Broadway. The studio was located on the second floor of a loft at 207

Broadway, and from the building plans we know that Brady had carpenters build skylights in the roof. He may have had the idea from visiting Morse's "glass palace" which the inventor had constructed on the roof of the University of the City of New York (now New York University) in 1840. Brady, together with Page, also had visited Morse at the inventor's second "sun palace" built for him by his brothers, Sidney and Richard, on the roof of the building they owned on the northeast corner of Nassau and Beekman Streets. The more sunlight, the better type of Daguerreotype could be produced, Morse insisted.

Brady must have opened his gallery some time in early 1844 because in the spring, when the American Institute held its first competitive photographic exhibition, Brady walked off with the silver medal for first honors. In the next four years Brady won the same prize. In fact, it became so monotonous that *Humphrey's Journal*, one of the early Daguerrean trade periodicals, announced with a casual air, "Mr. B. has won again."

In those days Brady was an aggressive, personable young man of little formal education and with a bad case of myopia. While he continued to make commercial Daguerreotypes he was also persuading prominent Americans to sit for him. In 1848 Mrs. Dolley Madison consented to pose for him in her home on Lafayette Square just off Madison Place and H Street, Washington. A year later she died at the age of eighty-one.

Mrs. Alexander Hamilton, then ninety-one years old, George Washington Parke Custis, the master of Arlington House on the Virginia side of the Potomac River, and Chief Justice Roger B. Taney, all sat for Brady in 1848.

Brady's studio was an immediate success. While he took hundreds of thousands of commercial Daguerreotypes he also initiated a pictorial historical project of enormous scope. He wanted to photograph just about every important historical personage: presidents, generals, soldiers, heroes, statesmen. These were intended for an impressive volume to be called *Gallery of Illustrious Americans,* or as Brady once termed

BRA 47 BRA

Brady James, laborer, 97 Reade
Brady James, grocer, 102 Cherry
Brady James, carman, 83 Lewis
Brady James, clothier, 68 Liberty
Brady James, runner emig. hotel, 31 Bridge
Brady James, carpenter, 82 Orange
Brady James, porterhouse, 236 Division
Brady James, laborer, 15 Pearl
Brady James B. grocer, 541 Grand
Brady James T. lawyer, 27 Beekman, h. 538 Houston
Brady Jemima, widow of Jesse, 133 Amos
Brady John, measurer, 130 W. Sixteenth
Brady John, joiner, 131 Willett
Brady John, shoemaker, r. 46 Hester
Brady John, grocer, 397 Grand
Brady John, huckster, Essex mkt. h. 67 Ludlow
Brady John, waiter, r. 116 Duane
Brady John, polisher, — Broadway, h. 219 Mulberry
Brady John, porter, 15 Pearl
Brady John, lamplighter, r. 14 Ridge
Brady John, laborer, 6 Batavia
Brady John, mason, r. 4 Goerck
Brady John, printer, 288 Mulberry
Brady John B. porter Greenwich bank, h. 133 Amos
Brady John R. lawyer, 27 Beekman, h. 538 Houston
Brady John S. butcher, Bank c. Hudson, h. 128 Amos
Brady John W. butcher, r. 49 Essex
Brady Joseph, carpenter, 9 Orange, h. 131 White
Brady Josiah R. 85 Houston
Brady Lewis, staircaser, 119 Perry
Brady Margaret, widow of James, 38 Sheriff
Brady Margaret, wid. Barney, 425 West c. Hammond
Brady Margaret, widow of John S. 246 Division
Brady Mary, widow of John, liquors, 64 Prince
Brady Mary, widow of Josiah R. 5 St. John's lane
BRADY MATTHEW B. jewel, miniature, and surgical case manufacturer, 187 B'way, opposite John: Also Daguerrian miniature gallery 207 B'way, c. Fulton, entrance 162 Fulton, h. 63 Barclay
Brady Michael, grocer, 40 Frankfort
Brady Michael, laborer, 41 Pitt
Brady Michael, flagger, 273 Division
Brady Nancy, wid. Hugh, porter h. Av. 4 c. E. 17th
Brady Nicholas, carman, 46 Lewis
Brady Owen, carman, r. 271 Madison
Brady Patrick, machinist, 546 Fourth
Brady Patrick, wheelwright, 112 Houston
Brady Patrick, laborer, r. 122 Norfolk
Brady Patrick, laborer, 297 Monroe
Brady Patrick, laborer, h. 52 Cherry
Brady Patrick, milk, 18 Av. A.
Brady Patrick, laborer, r. 33 Monroe
Brady Patrick, grocer, 189 Varick, h. 63 King
Brady Patrick J. physician, 330 Broome
Brady Patrick S. grocer, 91 Bayard & 268 Stanton, h. 268 Stanton
Brady Peter, porter, 152 Leonard
Brady Philip, carman, Third n. Av. B.
Brady Philip, carpenter, 38 Av. B.
Brady Reuben, blacksmith, 525 Hudson, h. 30 Av. 8
Brady Rose, widow of James, 184 Second
Brady Samson, watchmaker, 106 Monroe
Brady Sybil, (col'd) widow Lewis, w. ct. Jackson row, in W. 22d n. Av. 6
Brady Terence, gratesetter, 77 Crosby
Brady Thomas, tailor, h. 84 Centre
Brady Thomas, carman, 709 Water
Brady Thomas, ragman, 167 Broome
Brady Thomas, laborer, 15 Willett
Brady William, barber, 80 Nassau
Brady William S. carman, 9 Cornelia
Brady Wm. V. silversmith, 48 Maiden l. h. 33 Bleecker
Brady A. & G. W. foundry, 72 Charles
Brady & Landon, porterhouse, r. 9 Frankfort
BRADY & MAURICE, lawyers, 27 Beekman
Brady, Anderson & Co. clothiers, 68 Liberty
Braem Elizabeth, widow of Rudolph, 24 Clinton pl.
Bragaldi Mario, artist, 348 Bowery
Bragg Alexis, boots and shoes, 269 Pearl, h. Brooklyn
Bragg Appleton, boots, &c. 269 Pearl, h. 137 Madison
Bragg Benson, carpenter, 62 Roosevelt
Bragg Franklin L. clerk, h. 35 Madison
Bragg George F. dry goods, 5 William & 1 S. Wm. h Franklin House
Bragg Henry T. teacher, 78 Crosby
Bragg Isaac F. teacher, 78 Crosby
Bragg Maynard, boots, &c. 295½ Pearl, h. 133 Prince
Bragg A. & Co. boots & shoes, 269 Pearl
Bragg & Whittemore, dry goods, 5 William & 1 S. Wm
Brahe A. H. tanner & currier, 27 Ferry, h. Brooklyn
Brahms John R. grocer, 303 Bowery, c. First
Braid George, pattern maker, 102 Lewis
Braidwood Thos. calico designer, 7 Merchants' ct.
Brainard Austin, physician, B'way, n. Twentieth
Brainard Elsey, boarding, 128 Division
Brainard Roswell C. 68 Fulton, h. Brooklyn
Brainard Samuel S. hardware, 308 Grand
Brainard William, mer. 154 Pearl, h. 161 W. 21st
Braine James H. com. mer. 96 Pine, h. 21 Frankfort
Braine John J. (Rev.) 205 Av. 8
Brainerd Amasa, jeweler, r. 5 Dey, h. 77 Varick
Brainerd Benjamin C. agent, 7 South, h. Brooklyn
Brainerd George W. distiller, 176 Front, h. 33 Jay
Brainerd Sam. S. hardware, 146 Bowery, h. 310 Broome
Brainerd Simeon, cabinetm'kr, 52 B'way, h. Brooklyn
Brainerd S. & H. Herkner, cabinetmakers, 52 B'way
Brainerd & Geffroy, jewelers, r. 5 Dey
Braislen John, carpenter, 120 Twelfth
Braisted Abram, refectory, 95 Hammond
Braisted Garret, seaman, r. 352 Front
Braisted Garret, oysters, Jef. mkt. h. 143 Waverly pl
Braisted Jacob, u. s. hotel, Water c. Fulton
Braisted John, 23 Lewis
Braisted John W. baker, 83 Av. D. & 388 Monroe, h. 388 Monroe
Braisted John W. jeweller, 482 Cherry
Braisted Peter, oysterhouse, 53 Hudson
Braisted Peter D. broker, 36 Fulton, h. 21 Christopher
Braisted Thos. H. broker, 190 Chatham, h. 23 Lewis
Braisted William C. broker, 59 Bowery, h. 26½ Lewis
Braisted & Johnson, u. s. h. Water, c. Fulton & Pearl
Braitmayer J. F. porterhouse, 72 Chrystie
Brake William, baker, Twelfth c. Avenue 1
Braman Jarvis, baths, 4 Cortlandt
Bramhall E. C. clerk, 35 Nassau, h. Jersey City
Bramhall Moses B. mer. 35 Nassau, h. Jersey City
BRAMHALL, ABERNETHY & COLLINS, drygds., 35 Nassau
Bramson John, mer. 149 Cedar, h. 188 E. Broadway
Bran William, 41 Rutgers
Branch Thomas W. furniture, 56 B'way, h. 128 Forsyth
Branch William L. furniture, 56 Broadway
Brand Alfred, carman, 377 Ninth
Brand Amos, butcher, Av. 8, c. W. 18th, h. 93 W. 19th
Brand Christian, grocery, 35 Grand & 501 Broome, h. Av. 5 c. 13th
Brand Enoch, shoemaker, r. 77 Charlton
Brand Frederick A. segars, 106 Chatham, h. 35 City Hall place
Brand John, root beer, 103 Delancy
Brand John, second-hand goods, 182 Second
Brand John, butcher, W. 16th, c. Av. 9, h. 209 W. 16th
Brand John jr., butcher, Av 8 c. W. Nineteenth
Brand Rebecca N. teacher, 504 Broome
Brand Thomas, cartman, 377 Ninth
Brand William, importer, 42 Pine, h. Hoboken
Brand C. & Co. grocers, 35 Grand, 501 Broome & 13th c. Av. 5
Brand & Stegman, grocers, 501 Broome c. Laurens
Braudau Jacob, shoemaker, 85 Allen
Brandegee Jacob, 3 Leroy pl. Bleecker
Brandenburg Christian, tailor, 292 Washington
Brandes Elias, basket maker, 198 Division
BRANDRETH BENJ. pills, 241 B'way, 274 Bowery, & 241 Hudson
Brandreth James, woodsawyer, r. 43 Anthony
Brandon Joseph, broker, 28 Wall, h. 568 Broome
Brandon William, carman, 110 Mulberry
Brandt Clouse, grocer, 114 Monroe, h. 114 Monroe
Brandt Diedrick, grocer, 267 William, h. 267 William
Brandt & Steffen, grocers, 114 Monroe
Branen Michael, grocer, 50 Cherry
Branigan Patrick, paver, r. 246 Cherry
Branigan Terence, porterhouse, 31 Washington

New York Street Directory for 1844–45.

them, "the men and mothers of America." Included that winter of 1849–50 were photographs he took of John Quincy Adams, Clay, Calhoun, and Webster.

Brady continued to prosper in the 1850s. When woodcut illustrations became possible from Daguerreotypes, Brady became one of the leading contributors to *Harper's Weekly Magazine* and *Leslie's Illustrated Weekly.*

Brady undoubtedly overworked his naturally weak eyes during these years for we find references to his failing eyesight and the thick blue lenses he was forced to wear.[10]

As the *Photographic Art Journal* of 1851 pointed out:

"Mr. Brady is not operating himself. A failing eyesight precludes the possibility of his using

Downtown New York, 1848, showing Brady's Fulton Street Gallery, on the southwest corner of Fulton Street.

the camera with any certainty. But he is an excellent artist, nevertheless, understands his business perfectly and gathers around him the finest talent to be found . . ."

An undated newspaper clipping, probably from the New York *Herald,* also commented on Brady's failing sight and how he was forced to use tinted lenses in his glasses.

Brady by now was more a proprietor than an actual photographer. He had worked for years perfecting the new art, but once this mastery had been accomplished, he left the business of taking pictures to his operators. However, although he was making a great deal of money, he never relinquished good taste for financial gain. He was always ready to experiment and to purchase new equipment. His operators were the best. At one time he employed an operator who charged the unusually high fee of fifty dollars a lesson to learn the collodion process.

He was absent from his business for long periods—eighteen months at one time—but the quality of the work produced by his galleries never suffered. Brady was also deeply concerned about the "new art" which had given him such a good life. On January 15, 1855, he wrote to Samuel F. B. Morse, who had taught him the art of the Daguerreotype.

"The fact that it (photography) has found its way where other phases of artistic beauty would have been disregarded is recognized. During my experience, however, I have endeavored to render it as far as possible an auxiliary to the artist. While the other features of its develop-

Brady's award won in the American Institute Exhibition of 1844.

Brady's famous Daguerreotype of Dolley Madison. Scratched and damaged, yet still an invaluable link with America's past.

102.

Wednesday Feby 14th 1849: The number of persons, male and female who called this morning was unusually great, and the importunate applications for office, were exceedingly annoying. The impression has obtained that Genl. Taylor, may possibly not be proscriptive, — and the herd of persons who are without political principle — and who are willing to profess to belong to either party, to obtain or hold office, — are anxious to get in before I retire, in the hope that they will not be turned out after I retire. I have great contempt for such persons, and dispose of their applications very summarily. They take up much of my time every day. — I yielded to the request of an artist named Brady of N.Y. by sitting for my Daguerreotype likeness to day. — I sat in the large dining-room. I disposed of business on

A page from John Quincy Adams' diary, with the notation of his "sitting" for Brady on Wednesday, February 14, 1849.

ment have not been disregarded I have esteemed this of paramount importance. How far I have succeeded and whether the recognition among artists has been commensurate with the aid they have derived from it I know of none so eminently qualified to judge as yourself . . ."[11]

However, although Brady recognized the artistic possibilities of photography, he was still the proprietor, the owner, the businessman. As Professor Robert Taft points out, "One judges the artist by the work of his own hand, not by the work turned out by his employees. This is not to say that some of the work turned out by Brady's studios may not have artistic value, but in most cases we do not know who deserves the praise for such merit."[12]

Brady, like many New York gallery owners, insisted that his name be stamped on every Daguerreotype or paper print, no matter what operator took the picture. But this was not unusual. John Plumbe, Jr., who had opened his first gallery in 1841 and who soon had a chain of fourteen from New York to St. Louis, insisted that everything coming from his studio be stamped "Plumbe." This pattern was soon accepted, and today with few exceptions it is virtually impossible to determine the operator who took the specific picture.

We do not know what photographs or Daguerreotypes O'Sullivan took under Brady. It would be the Scot, Alexander Gardner, who would give him credit for the photographs he would take in the Civil War and fortunately the later government reports include his name under his photographs.

In the late forties or early fifties Brady married. His wife is a shadowy figure, a placid-looking woman with thick, sausage-like curls staring into a camera. Although her given name appears on legal documents as Juliette R. C. Handy, she was called Julia all her life. A few yellowing clippings give her kinship to a number of aristocratic Eastern Shore and Virginia families. They remained childless.

With his eyesight failing badly and his business booming Brady took his wife on a grand tour of Europe. He was gone eighteen months and left behind in charge George S. Cook, who may have been the famous Confederate photographer.

While he was abroad the development of the wet plate revolutionized photography. In 1851 Frederick Scott Archer, an English sculptor, announced his process of using collodion as an agent to keep the image on the glass plate. Collodion was a sticky liquid made by dissolving nitrated cotton in a mixture of alcohol and ether. The ether and alcohol, evaporating rapidly, left behind the smooth transparent film which was sensitized by bathing in a solution of silver nitrate. The plate had to be used when wet or damp because the sensitivity was lost when the plate dried. The wet plates were developed by a solution of ferrous (iron) sulphate made acid with acetic acid. Potassium cyanide fixed the plate.

The wet plate at first made little impact in New York but by the time Brady had returned

Brady and his wife and her sister. Left to right, Mrs. Brady, Mathew Brady, and Mrs. Haggerty, in the late 1850s.

the *Photographic Art Journal* was describing Archer's methods and some operators were experimenting with the new process. *Humphrey's Journal* pointed out that a certain skill had to be developed to coat the plate properly and that "the initial results were uncertain."

The prints of the period were made on paper dipped into a common salt solution—"salted paper"—and were dull and lifeless. However, albumen was soon added which provided a glossy finished look to the prints.

By 1852–53 the Daguerreotype was dying fast and the era of paper photography had begun. Brady, Gurney, Lawrence, Anthony, and the rest, their business volume increasing, opened larger and more luxurious quarters.

In addition to his gallery at Broadway and Fulton Street, Brady opened others on Fulton Street, Brooklyn, Broadway and Prince Street, and his most famous "uptown" gallery at Broadway and Tenth Street, "Over Thompson's Saloon," which he called Brady's Famous National Portrait Gallery.

The latter was the largest and most ornate of all of Brady's galleries. Humphrey, the pioneer photographic trade journalist, paid a visit to it and left behind an excellent description in his *Journal* of Daguerreotypes, June 15, 1853. At the door, he wrote, was a series of showcases in rosewood and gilt frames. Up two flights the customers entered the reception rooms through doors of figured glass. Inside, velvet tapestry hung from the ceiling to the floor, walls glowed with gold and silver paper, and hanging from the ceiling in the middle of the room was a huge chandelier of cut crystal that sparkled like imprisoned stars in the mellow gaslight. Only curtains of the finest needlework hung from the windows "to diffuse the light." Scattered about the room were rosewood chairs, tête-à-têtes, gleaming marble tables, and banks of mirrors. There was a special "Ladies Parlor," papered with green and satin. Rosewood and fragile gilt-painted chairs lined the room.

There was a rapid turnover in operators; they came and they went from the Broadway studios. Many are just names, others made immortal pictures for Brady, such as Polycarp von Schneidau, who took Jenny Lind's picture and the unforgettable Chicago picture of Lincoln.

44 BROADWAY, STREET DIRECTORY.

Here Leonard st. intersects.

847 Spencer & Doty, lawyers. (Charles S. Spencer, J. V. W. Doty)
Francis Henocque, lawyer
JOHN H. VAN DOLAR, perfumery
N. P. Munger, sewing machines
Phineas Freeman, sewing machines
Philips & Davis, lawyers, (Alfred A. Philips, Burton H. Davis)
Chester B. Howes, real estate agent
Henry C. Rowe, teacher penmanship
Cornelius Burling, lawyer
Fernando Rodriguez, lawyer
Joseph Wood, real estate broker
Myron H. Kimball, ambrotypes, &c
James Panton, shirt bosom manuf.
Alex. C. Lawrence, real estate broker
Samuel E. Boyer, lightning rods

847 Bernard E. Meyer, com. mer.
H. Hudson, com. mer.
John Crumby, fine arts
Napoleon B. Gosling, restaurant
849 John Cox & Co. gas fixtures. (Alfred H. Cox, Joseph Cox, Henry T. Cox)
Roberts & Hankey, dining saloon. (Samuel Roberts, Henry Hankey)
WILEY & HALSTED, imps., & publishers. (John Wiley, Robert Halsted)
American Institute. (John W. Chambers, sec.)
850 & 52 S. B. Chittenden
853 WILLIAMS, STEVENS, WILLIAMS & CO. looking glass & picture frames. (John H. Williams, Linus W. Stevens, George H. Williams, John McClure)
854 JOHN R. LAWRENCE & CO. carriage makers. (Stephen A. Durbrow)
855 STRANG, ADRIANCE & CO. drygds. (Theodosius Strang, James B. Adriance, Stephen B. Strang, John McMurtie)

356 Janes, Beebe & Co. furnaces ranges, &c. (Adrian Janes William Beebe, Charle, Fowler, Charles A. Kirtland, Edward R. Janes, George Janes)
Israel B. Cohen, segar mkr.
Capewell & Kimmel, engravers, historical. (Sam'l Capewell, Christopher Kimmel)
A. Ward & Co. map & print colorers. (Albert Ward, Capewell & Kimmel)
359 Thompson & Son, restaurant. (James Thompson, Lucas Thompson)
M. B. BRADY, imperial photograph, daguerreotype & ambrotype gallery
360 Kimball, Whittemore & Co looking-glass manufs.
John J. Staff, wines & liquors, impporter of
JOHN D. CHEVALIER, dental ins. & materials
George W. Pratt, (assignee) paperhangings
Albert G. Richardson, advertising agent

Thompson's Saloon

Brady's "uptown" Broadway gallery "over Thompson's saloon" as it appeared in Boyd's Pictorial Directory of Broadway, 1859.

By now Brady was famous both in the United States and abroad. His customers were the celebrities of the world and he was on first-name basis with every important politician, statesman, and general in Washington. In the first World's Fair in London—"Albert's Fair," as Victoria called it—he took the silver medal for his collection of Daguerreotypes. The new honors brought more attention. Money was pouring in, his reputation was established, his collection of historic pictures growing. Brady's laurels were never fresher, never greener.

An interior view of Brady's "uptown" gallery at Broadway and Tenth Street.

It was about this time that Brady, his eyesight fading and his business expanding, began casting about for a general manager who could take care of both his New York studio and a contemplated gallery in Washington.

This would not be Brady's first Washington venture as it has been believed. In 1849 he opened "Daguerrean rooms" at Four-and-One-Half Street above the jewelry store owned and operated by Charles W. Heydon. According to the records of the local Circuit Court, Brady had to obtain an injunction to prevent Heyden from evicting him from his quarters. Shortly after the court action Brady abandoned Washington to return to New York.[13]

In the early fifties he selected Alexander Gardner, a bearded Scot from Paisley, Scotland, who was to be an important figure in O'Sullivan's life. Gardner's mother came from a long line of ministers, landowners, and physicians. We know little about his father. When he was fourteen he became a jeweler's apprentice and kept the job for seven years while he studied chemistry and astronomy at night. When he had finished his school he left for Glasgow to become a reporter on the Glasgow *Sentinel*. By 1848 he was editor-in-chief.

Gardner, one of the first students of the Pitman system of shorthand, an avid follower of Robert Owen's labor reforms—trade unions, ed-

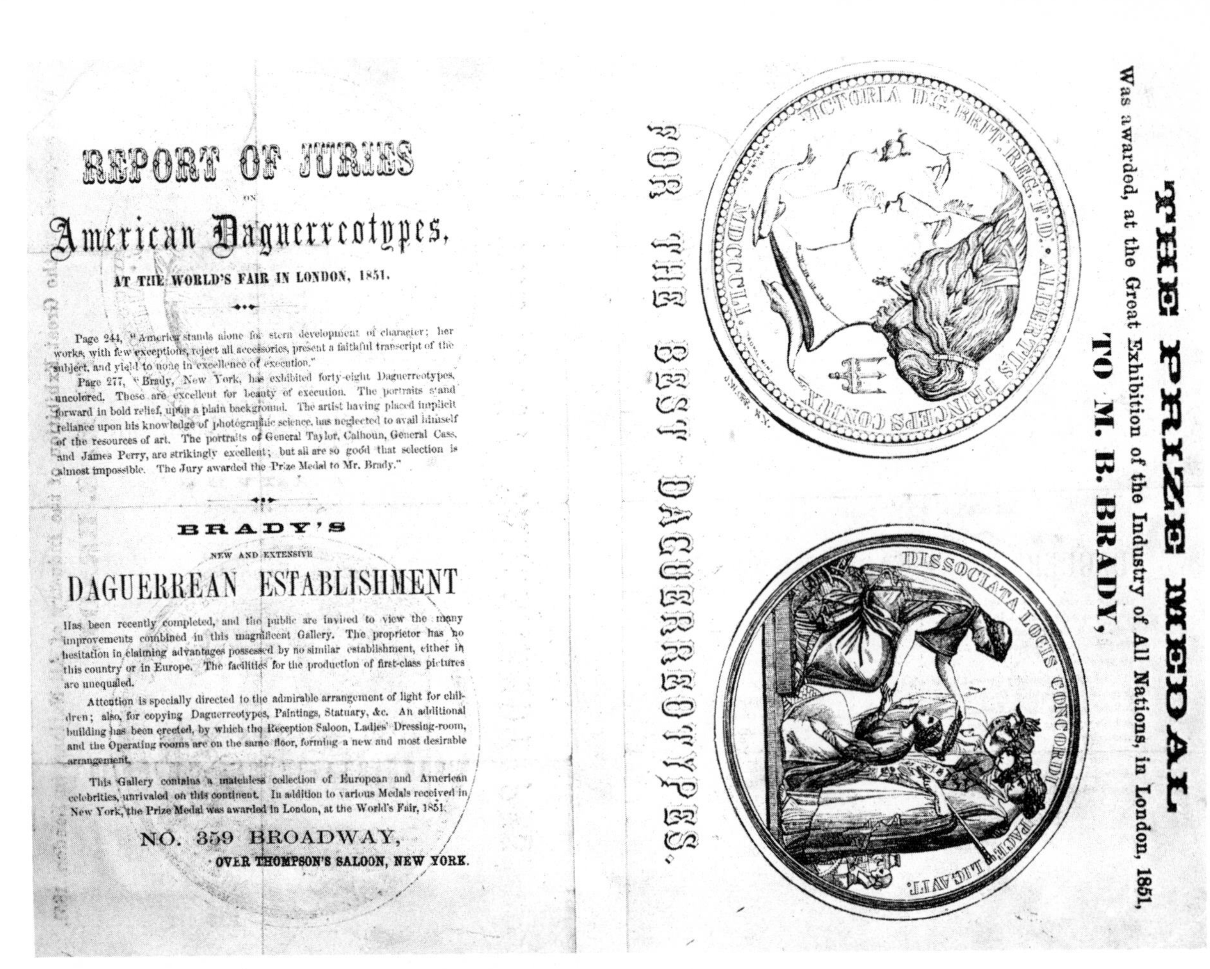
REPORT OF JURIES

ON

American Daguerreotypes,

AT THE WORLD'S FAIR IN LONDON, 1851.

Page 244, "America stands alone for stern development of character; her works, with few exceptions, reject all accessories, present a faithful transcript of the subject, and yield to none in excellence of execution."

Page 277, "Brady, New York, has exhibited forty-eight Daguerreotypes, uncolored. These are excellent for beauty of execution. The portraits stand forward in bold relief, upon a plain background. The artist having placed implicit reliance upon his knowledge of photographic science, has neglected to avail himself of the resources of art. The portraits of General Taylor, Calhoun, General Cass, and James Perry, are strikingly excellent; but all are so good that selection is almost impossible. The Jury awarded the Prize Medal to Mr. Brady."

BRADY'S

NEW AND EXTENSIVE

DAGUERREAN ESTABLISHMENT

Has been recently completed, and the public are invited to view the many improvements combined in this magnificent Gallery. The proprietor has no hesitation in claiming advantages possessed by no similar establishment, either in this country or in Europe. The facilities for the production of first-class pictures are unequaled.

Attention is specially directed to the admirable arrangement of light for children; also, for copying Daguerreotypes, Paintings, Statuary, &c. An additional building has been erected, by which the Reception Saloon, Ladies' Dressing-room, and the Operating rooms are on the same floor, forming a new and most desirable arrangement.

This Gallery contains a matchless collection of European and American celebrities, unrivaled on this continent. In addition to various Medals received in New York, the Prize Medal was awarded in London, at the World's Fair, 1851.

NO. 359 BROADWAY,

OVER THOMPSON'S SALOON, NEW YORK.

THE PRIZE MEDAL

Was awarded, at the Great Exhibition of the Industry of All Nations, in London, 1851,

TO M. B. BRADY,

FOR THE BEST DAGUERREOTYPES.

Brady's prize medal, World's Fair, 1851.

ucation, socialist communities—came to the United States in 1849 to establish one of Owen's "Cooperative societies" on the Mississippi in Iowa. Several months later he returned to Glasgow and his newspaper job. However, he continued to write pamphlets, lecture, and recruit other settlers. In 1856 he planned to bring his family to Iowa but en route he heard the news that many settlers in the frontier community were dying of "galloping consumption." Leaving his family behind in a frontier settlement he rushed to Iowa to help an orphaned niece and his friends. When they had recovered he returned to his family. Shortly after, they left for New York City.

How Brady hired him is not known. Legend has Brady meeting him during his European tour. Gardner, according to the trade journals of his time, was already "an accomplished photographer" so probably he sought out one of the most popular studios in the city and Brady, recognizing an intelligent expert, hired him.

In the late 1850s Gardner took over as manager of the Brady National Photographic Art Gallery, 350–352 Pennsylvania Avenue (now 625–627), and brought along his brother, James, as an assistant.

The gallery occupied three upper stories of a building that housed Gilman's Drug Store and the banking house of Sweeney, Rittenhouse and Fant. One door east, in a five-story building over Todd, the hatter, and Galt, the jeweler, was Plumbe's gallery. An article in a Washington newspaper complimented Brady for his "photographic exhibition of fair women and grave and reverent seignors . . . those who have not yet seen this charming gallery would do well to while away an hour in scanning this array of beauty, diplomacy, living senatorial and clerical celebrity besides the speaking, almost startling likenesses of the great ones who have departed this earth . . ."[14]

The Brady gallery encountered lively competition in Washington from Plumbe, and the other operators whose galleries lay in a cluster in the area of Pennsylvania Avenue between Third Street and Market Space. His prices were well above those of his competitors but Brady had a shrewd public relations sense and he kept his name before the public as much as possible.

When Gardner appeared in Washington he introduced the stylish "imperials," life-size enlargements from copies of Daguerreotypes finished in India ink. These enlargements—sometimes greeted with a sneer by his competitors—were made with a Woodward Solar Camera and measured 17 by 21 inches.

Brady allowed Gardner to operate with a free hand; apparently his theory was not to interfere as long as the gallery made money. Before the opening of the Civil War, Brady would occasionally visit Washington, staying at the fashionable hotels, like the National House, Brown's Indian Queen, and the American House, all on Pennsylvania Avenue. A social event could also attract the Bradys to the capital. In 1858 as the artist Van Dyke he attended the fashionable costume ball given by Senator William McKendree Gwin of Mississippi in his fashionable house at Third and C Streets.

Brady's gallery was elaborate, probably one of the most elaborate in Washington. Property inventories required by the court in the course of bankruptcy proceedings against him in later years gives a hint of the luxurious interior.[15]

The second-floor reception room, actually the gallery's showplace, was opened every day except Sunday. Along the walls were portraits of world-famous figures, American statesmen, entertainers. In showcases at the street entrance were samples of the gallery's photographic work, usually prominent residents of Washington.

To soothe impatient customers was a large wooden box for the viewing of stereoscopic slides, Niagara Falls, European scenes, French comics.

Above the reception room was the finishing room and the mounting room, where the art work was done, albumen prints retouched and finished in oils, crayons, water colors. The negatives were not touched except for an occasional thin strip of white paper pasted to the negative to whiten a sky area. Pictures were framed with arabesque walnut or gilt. Cases for the prints were known as ovals or jewels, or Jenny Linds or Cupids. In the mounting room were two presses, a large and a small one, along with mats, cards, and racks.

The actual operators worked on the top floor of the gallery to catch the direct sunlight through the skylight. The customers entering this room saw two cameras, four headrests, three chairs for posing the subject—one a child's—two tables, a French plate-glass mirror, a marble stand, a clock, a painted screen, a bronze

Alexander Gardner, an oil portrait by Charles Armor.

An early interior of a Broadway photographic gallery in the 1850s. Photographer unknown.

cloth for forming draperies, reflectors, screens, pedestals, an Italian vase, a footrest, and a stove. Off to one side in the vestibule was a desk, safe, chair, and a spittoon.

A dressing room was provided for customers wishing to make the final touches. Here was a marble-top washstand, washbowl, pitcher, towel rack, chair. The room was carpeted.

The real working room was the darkroom. Here were the usual bath dishes and dippers, trimming glass, an extension tube for the cameras, stacks of glass plates of various sizes, assorted chemicals, frames, lacquered metal and copper plates, a set of scales, and a gas oven for drying negatives.

Appointments were made for the morning

Cutting and mounting stereo room of an 1850 gallery. Photographer unknown.

only. Rain canceled them. On cloudy days longer exposures were needed, undoubtedly causing much impatience among the customers in the reception room who had wearied of staring into the wooden box and seeing more slides of European cities and Niagara Falls.

There were two apprentice photographers. The artists were the highest paid, mostly by the day. Their scale was eleven dollars a day and $16.66 for Sunday work. The women who did the mounting and framing received eight dollars a week.

Gardner's props were a gold clock which never changed the time—ten minutes to twelve—a leather-bound copy of *The Annals of Congress,* a fringed Gothic chair, a Sarony chair

Typical family group posing for a Daguerreotype in the late 1850s in Brady's studio. As an apprentice O'Sullivan helped to "pose" such groups.

This is the type of house in which O'Sullivan lived in West Brighton, Staten Island, near the Brady residence.

BRA 99 BRA

Brady John, police, h 177 W. 47th
Brady John, porter, h 315 Ninth
Brady John, produce, 110 W. Wash. mkt
Brady John, seaman, h r 118 Wash'n
Brady John, tailor, h r 49 Lewis
Brady John, teacher, h 257 E. 17th
Brady John, watchman, h r 845 Seventh av.
Brady John jr. police, h 185 W. 89th
Brady John jr. produce, 110 W. Wash. mkt
Brady John H. builder, 122 Amity, & alderman, h 136 Amity
Brady John J. clerk, h 161 E. 45th
Brady John L. jeweler, h 457 Fourth av.
Brady John R. judge com. pleas, 13 City Hall, h 124 W. 23d
Brady Joseph C. carpenter, E. 56th n Second av. h E. 55th n Third av.
Brady Lucy E. millinery, Third av. n E. 126th
Brady Margaret, candy, h 246 Mott
Brady Margaret, confectioner, Third av. n E. 117th
Brady Margaret, wid. Charles, h 169 E. 16th
Brady Margaret, wid. Foster, h 78 Henry
Brady Margaret, wid. James, h 170 E. 16th
Brady Martin, laborer, h 266 E. 12th
Brady Martin, mason, h 293 W. 27th
Brady Mary, drygds, h 506 Second av.
Brady Mary, huckster, 52 Centre mkt
Brady Mary, liquors, 123 E. 26th
Brady Mary, liquors, h 64 E. 39th
Brady Mary, strawhats, h 112 W. 19th
Brady Mary, washing, h 45 W. 41st
Brady Mary, wid. Edward, washing, h 216 Canal
Brady Mary, wid. James, liquors, 517 Pearl
Brady Mary, wid. Matthew, pants, h 78 Cannon
Brady Mary, wid. Patrick, dressmkr, h r 634 Hudson
Brady Mary, wid. Thomas, h 14 Ridge
Brady Mary, wid. William, h E. 127th n Third av.
Brady Mary L. wid. Josiah, h 218 Varick
Brady Matthew, clerk, h 297 E. 14th
Brady Matthew, junk, h 298 W. 18th
Brady Matthew, laborer, h r 167 W. 33d
Brady Matthew, rags, 79 Willett, h 78 Willett
Brady Matthew B. photographer, 643 B'way, h S. I.
Brady Michael, broker, 108 South, h 715 Eighth av.
Brady Michael, carman, h W. 50th n Ninth av.
Brady Peter, plasterer, h 251 E. 18th
Brady Peter, produce, 110 W. Wash. mkt, h J. C.
Brady Philip, carpenter, h 187 W. 27th
Brady Philip, grocer, 93 Monroe
Brady Philip, flagger, h 158 W. 32d
Brady Philip, laborer, 61 Leandert's pl.
Brady Philip, laborer, h r 204 W. 42d
Brady Philip, pickles, 67½ Ludlow
Brady Philip, wheelwright, h 205 E. 32d
Brady Philip J. ribbons, 55 Walker, h 170 E. 21st
Brady Reuben, smith, 625 Hudson, h 340 W. 12th
Brady Richard, grocer, 20 Roosevelt
Brady Richard, mason, h 331 Bowery
Brady Rosanna, wid. Thomas, h 40 Sheriff
Brady Rose, wid. George, fancygds, 814 Ninth
Brady Rose, wid. Hugh, h 354 First av.
Brady Rose, wid. John, h 178 E. 32d
Brady Stephen J. lawyer, 76 Wall, h 72 Henry
Brady Terence, laborer, h 145 W. 41st
Brady Terence J. liquors, 22 Beaver, h 69 Pike
Brady Terence P. h 164 Seventh av.
Brady Theodore W. smith, h 1192 B'way
Brady Thomas, boardingh. 129 Cedar
Brady Thomas, butcher, 20 Rutgers
Brady Thomas, carman, h 233 Delancey
Brady Thomas, carman, h 362 Madison
Brady Thomas, carman, h 200 W. 42d
Brady Thomas, contractor, h 845 Third av.
Brady Thomas, cooper, h 220 Tenth av.
Brady Thomas, furrier, h 57 W. 44th
Brady Thomas, junk, 212 Monroe, h 218 Monroe
Brady Thomas, laborer, 330½ Cherry
Brady Thomas, laborer, h r 95 E. 11th
Brady Thomas, laborer, h r 98 Norfolk
Brady Thomas, laborer, h r 48 Oliver
Brady Thomas, laborer, h 56 Roosevelt
Brady Thomas, laborer, h 504 Tenth av.
Brady Thomas, laborer, h r 522 Wash'n
Brady Thomas, laborer, h 275 W. 39th
Brady Thomas, liquors, 87 Willett
Brady Thomas, porter, h 44 Mulberry
Brady Thomas H. liquors, 24 West, h 150 Plymouth, B'klyn
Brady Thomas L. boardingh. 326 Pearl
Brady Walter, broker, 8 Pine, h Fifth av. c W. 129th

New York Street Directory showing Brady's Staten Island address. Until this was found it was purely legend—many times denied by historians—that Brady had ever lived in this section. The directory shows he first came to the island in 1859 and lived there until the 1870s, when he fled to Washington one jump ahead of the U. S. Marshal. Brady had moved cartloads of goods from his New York gallery just before its contents were taken for auction.

with removable arms, and a Corinthian column. The last was valuable for standing poses.

Turned around it turned out to be an Ionic column. About the floor were sockets for the body rests, an essential part of the early photographer's equipment. It held the subject's head rigid and supported his spine.

If a customer was waiting in the reception room when Brady made one of his occasional visits, he would see a slender, medium-sized man, dressed in a black coat, black doeskin trousers and a merino vest, tailor-made for him at the fashionable Bellantoni's. His shirt was the finest muslin, his scarf silk, his handkerchief linen. He sported a cane, and tucked inside his coat were extra pairs of spectacles. The customer's nose might twitch as he passed; Brady used only the best lotions, and Lubin or Windsor's soap, lavender water, or Atwood's cologne.

In this gallery O'Sullivan would spend the next few years as a photographer under Gardner, after serving his apprenticeship in Brady's New York gallery.

Legend has Brady knowing O'Sullivan as a boy. One of the few existing Brady letters confirms he knew O'Sullivan "from boyhood," while vital statistics, deeds, and newspapers of the time link them in the same neighborhood.

A deed in 1853 reveals O'Sullivan's father, Jeremiah, bought a home in Castleton Corners, Staten Island, then also known as Grymes Hill, where Brady had a home, variously described as a "mansion" or a "cottage." One Staten Island weekly of the time, *The Gazette*, congratulated Brady on choosing Staten Island for his home and Doggett's city directory shows that Brady lived on the Island from 1853—when O'Sullivan's father bought his house—to 1861 when he moved to the National Hotel in Washington to direct his photographic coverage of the Civil War.

We know the artist William Page, who persuaded Brady to come to New York, lived on Staten Island during the 1840s—prior to leaving for Europe in 1849—and it is not unreasonable to assume Brady first came there with him.[16]

Staten Island at the time was a delightful country place of rolling farms, fine homes, and forest land. It is not generally known that it was also the home and gathering place for many men who helped to shape the rapidly growing world of photography.

One towering giant in the world of the "new art" was Dr. John William Draper who lived on Cherry Lane, now Forrest Avenue, Staten Island, at the time of Daguerre's announcement to the world. Son of a Wesleyan clergyman, Draper had been writing articles and contributing scientific essays to the Rees Encyclopaedia while he was still in his teens. In 1832 he came to the United States from England and lived in Virginia for a time. Five years later, at twenty-six, he was appointed head of the Chemistry Department of the University of the City of New York. It is believed he moved to Staten Island about that time.

Draper had been keenly interested in the solar system and when Daguerre's announcement stirred the world, he was conducting experiments to ascertain the effects of different kinds of light upon chemical changes.

Draper made the first photographic portrait of a human face of which copies are known to exist, probably late in 1839. As Draper later explained, he coated the face of his sister with white powder, but after a few experiments he decided that was not necessary. On March 20, 1840, he displayed his portrait of his sister at the Lyceum of Natural History of New York. The Daguerreotype, one inch in diameter, had been taken on a brilliant day with a twenty-minute exposure.

Draper's close friend was Howard J. Chilton, another Staten Islander, whose apothecary shop was on the southwest corner of Fourth and Wooster, near the University where Draper taught. Chilton, probably through Draper's influence, also opened a Daguerreotype gallery. It

Dr. John William Draper, another Staten Island resident, experimented with photography two years before the Daguerreotype was announced.

John Draper's portrait of his sister Dorothy, taken in 1840. This is the earliest photographic portrait of which copies still exist.

was Chilton who made photographic history when he put on display in his window D. W. Seager's Daguerreotype of St. Paul's Church and a corner of the Astor House, the first successful Daguerreotype made in the United States. On September 30, 1839, the readers of the *Morning Herald* read about the amazing picture and crowds flocked to Chilton's to see the new marvel. A few days later, as the result of his new-found fame, Seager, an Englishman, inserted in the *Herald* the first known photographic advertisement. Morse and Draper are listed as his sponsors.

Another little-known pioneer photographer, Charles E. Hoyer, had a photographic studio in Staten Island's Planter's Hotel. Hoyer's studio was later taken over by another excellent photographer, John Loeffler, later joined by his son, August.

The studio and photographic wagon of John E. Lake, early Staten Island photographer. By J. E. Lake.

One of the most picturesque photographers of the Island, and who undoubtedly was known to O'Sullivan in the postwar years, was John E. Lake, who traveled about the country roads with a horse and wagon—curiously, a traveling darkroom similar to the one which both Brady and O'Sullivan used in the Civil War.

In this small rural community these sophisticated, cosmopolitan men—Brady, Draper, Chilton and the others—were undoubtedly the subject of much conversation. There is nothing to tell us about O'Sullivan's early life, but is it not possible that they influenced his love of photography, perhaps even encouraged him, perhaps taught him?

A characteristic of the majority of the leading figures of early photography was their generosity, their desire to encourage others to enter the new art. We find Draper and Morse listed as sponsors for the Englishman Seager. And many years after the Civil War, Brady would recall how Draper "counseled" him when he was beginning . . .

One can imagine Brady, peering through his blue-tinted glasses as he carefully explained to the young farm boy from down the road, the basics of the camera obscura or how the plate had to slide into the wooden Daguerreotype camera . . .

O'Sullivan, a slender, good-looking boy, lived with his father, Jeremiah, and his mother, Ann. Like thousands of others they had left the rotting potato fields of Ireland in 1842 for the United States. Timothy at the time was two years old; there was a brother and sister of whom we know nothing.

More than ten years ago the late Mrs. Cox, Brady's niece and only survivor, told the author she "understood" O'Sullivan came to work for Brady "when he was a boy. Just picking up things and Mr. Brady taught him how to be a photographer."[17]

One can picture the country boy dodging the vegetable wagons and drays as he hurried off the *Josephine,* the Staten Island ferryboat, to swing up Broadway to Fulton Street—then the Times Square of New York. There were clanging horsecars, crowds, men in beavers, and ladies in dresses that swept the sidewalk. Barnum's Museum was close by and a block away was the

One of the earliest photos of the moon. This shot was publicized a great deal in the United States and Europe and undoubtedly was seen and discussed by Brady, O'Sullivan, and Gardner. Probably by John Adams Whipple who daguerreotyped an eclipse at Harvard College Observatory on July 28, 1851.

fashionable Astor House. The noise, confusion, and crowds must have been both exciting and breathtaking to this sensitive teenage country boy.

When Gardner took over as manager of the Washington gallery, O'Sullivan joined him.

In Washington he apparently demonstrated that he had served his New York apprenticeship well. The two Gardners, O'Sullivan, the women artists, and the bookkeeper whom Gardner insisted Brady hire made the gallery hum. Business was so good, Gardner hired Egbert Guy Fox, a Baltimore photographer, just before the war.

The gallery passed through the cycles of photography. Daguerreotypes gradually went out of fashion. The Gardners experimented with portraits. New and different cameras were tried and perfected. New techniques were used in enlarging, mounting, and finishing photographic prints.

Ambrotypes, basically a glass negative backed with black velvet or cardboard to make it positive and framed in the familiar Daguerreotype cases, became popular. In 1856, out of 123 wood engravings in *Frank Leslie's Illustrated Newspaper* for that year drawn from photographs, 100 were reproduced from ambrotypes, ten from paper photographs, and thirteen from Daguerreotypes.

Then the ambrotype lost its popularity to the tintype, also known in its day as the melainotype or ferrotype. It was a simple modification of the ambrotype. Instead of sensitizing and developing the glass negative, the tintype's inventor, Professor Hannibal L. Smith of Kenyon College, Gambier, Ohio, used a sheet of tin iron japanned black for the flowing collodion. Their lightness, toughness, and thin size—they could be sent through the mail—won them wide popularity and the tintype finally killed off the dying Daguerreotype. As Abraham Bogardus fondly wrote:

"I shall always remember with pleasure the good old Daguerreotype. No glass to clean or albumenize; no black fingers, few or no resittings; no retouching; no proofs to show for his grandmother and his sister, and his cousins, and his aunts to find fault with; no waiting for sunshine to print with; no paper to blister, and no promising of the pictures next week if the weather was good. The picture was gilded, finished and cased while the lady was putting on her bonnet; delivered and put in her pocket and you had the money in your pocket."[18]

The carte de visite was soon crowding the tintype for top popularity and from his negatives we know that O'Sullivan was highly proficient with the stereo camera, first conceived by a French photographer, Adolphe Eugene Disderi. His idea was to use a camera with four lenses to record several images on one plate.

Humphrey's Journal called the carte de visite "full length miniatures of the human face and form" and pointed out that a great deal of the beauty of the picture was obtained by the backgrounds which were used.

The small prints, mounted on cardboard, were used as a substitute for a calling card. The carte de visite may owe its origin to the Duke of Parma who started the fashion in 1857. The fad swept across Europe and spanned the Atlantic to become the new American craze.

The New York "Times Square" of 1859 which Tim O'Sullivan knew so well when he was working as an apprentice at Brady's Fulton Street Gallery. View was taken from Barnum's Museum. Brady's gallery was across the street. The park is the lower end of City Hall Park, Broadway is at the left. Photo by Anthony.

LEFT, *Gallery of Jeremiah Gurney, friend of Brady and O'Sullivan in 1854, at 349 Broadway, near Leonard Street. The picture was taken by Victor Provost in 1854. Provost was one of the best of the early photographers.* ABOVE, *Early rare view of an ambrotype wagon, 1850s.*

The first photograph taken from a balloon in 1861 with a wet plate, by Samuel A. King and J. W. Black.

Rare example of stereo made by Anthony in 1859. Anthony, founder of today's ANSCO, would supply O'Sullivan and Brady for their Civil War work and would also supply O'Sullivan for his Darién Expedition in 1870 and later Western surveys.

Brady saw the commercial possibilities immediately and set his staff producing cartes de visite by the bushel. Unskilled labor could cut up a single print, for which only the plate holder moved, into half a dozen portraits. Soon there wasn't an American home which did not have a "carte de visite basket" in the hall to collect photographs left by friends. Brady, the Anthonys, and all the other New York photographers produced millions. They begged, pleaded, and bribed sitters—actors, actresses, outlaws, mountain men, freaks, clergymen—anyone famous or infamous. The usual inducement was a small fee and a few copies of the print.

The New York operators had found the tintype more economical to produce than the Daguerreotype but now the stereo camera produced four or more negatives on one glass plate. The New York gallery owners, who never missed an opportunity to make a financial coup, saw the rapid production possibilities of the stereo camera and by 1860 Brady's New York and Washington studios were making hundreds of thousands of prints. Daguerreotypes were multiplied, Brady's Famous National Portrait Gallery was published by the Anthonys, and the public began collecting portraits of the famous. The stereo became the television of the American family of the Civil War era.

American photography had now grown to be an almost unbelievable commercial giant. Brady, the Anthonys, Jeremiah Gurney, and all the great New York photographers—the self-appointed aristocracy of American photography—were concerned only with gathering prizes and awards. Brady's luxurious new gallery on Broadway and Tenth Street was one of the showplaces of a city that reflected the gusto and extravagance of a lusty, restless America. Everything was out of size, out of drawing; six miles of roast pig lining Broadway in booths on a Fourth of July; champagne popping like firecrackers, ladies hats big as miniature windmills, Barnum's show always the "biggest, the greatest on earth!"; the new $100,000 mansion on Thirty-fourth Street built by Dr. Samuel T. Townsend, the sarsaparilla king . . . the more than $1,500,000 spent annually on the thoroughbreds at Saratoga . . .

These were years that the great figures of the world were coming to America, most of them to hurry to Brady's gallery to smile, wonder, sneer at this bumptious America. In October 1860 the Prince of Wales, later Edward VII, posed for Brady and had the photographer take him on a tour of his gallery of famous Americans. The impressed prince ordered copies of several and presented Brady with a cane, the silver head fashioned into a tiny camera.

But the days became uneasy. Soon the roar of war grew loud in the ears of the Republic. With the first shot the new art finally would find its destiny; in the hands of men like O'Sullivan, Gardner, and Brady, the fragile pieces of coated glass would soon imprison for history the violence, savagery, and havoc of the American Civil War.

One of the earliest known photographs of Lincoln by Brady.

3

THE CIVIL WAR

There is no doubt that while the noble purpose of Mathew B. Brady brought about the photographing of the Civil War, it was the aggressiveness, the heroism, and the photographic skill of Timothy H. O'Sullivan, Alexander Gardner and his brother Jim, J. J. Roche, Captain A. J. Russell, George M. Barnard, and the nameless others that produced a priceless heritage of photographs for countless generations of Americans.

O'Sullivan ranks as one of the most brilliant and the most sensitive photographers. One can almost feel the chilling mist as he set up his camera on the morning of the second day at Gettysburg to capture forever the magnificent sadness of the last of the Iron Brigade stiffened in death and stretching across the pasture as far as the camera's eye could see. In all his pictures of individuals we can sense the brave, the weary, the arrogant, the politician, the cynical veteran as they sprawl before a tent, lean on an overturned cannon or sit ramrod high in the saddle.

He left no record of his experiences. We find no letters to his wife, his mother, or his father. We can only trace him through his negatives, and the captions which he undoubtedly helped to prepare back in the Washington studio, and rebuild his life with the bits and pieces of vital statistics and official records.

Yet the story of how the Civil War was photographed must begin with Brady and his strange, almost spiritual determination to capture on glass the unforgettable conflict. Consider his motives, as he recalled them for Gath Townsend, the swashbuckling war correspondent of the New York *World,* twenty years after Appomattox:

"My wife and my most conservative friends had looked unfavorably upon this departure from commercial business, and I can only describe the destiny that overruled me by saying, like Euphorion, I felt I had to go. A spirit in me said 'go' and I went."[19]

Brady was not the first photographer to record a war. An unknown Daguerreotypist snapped General Woll and his troops in the Mexican War and Roger Fenton, an Englishman, had been sent out by Messrs. Agnew and Son of London to photograph the Crimea in 1855. Fenton's photographs, mostly of troops and scenes in and around Balaklava, cannot be compared in quality or scope to the work of Brady's men.

There is little doubt that Brady knew he was taking a desperate chance photographing the war. In addition to the personal dangers it would obviously mean his enormously successful commercial work would have to suffer. He now had palatial galleries scattered throughout New York City and in Washington. His eyesight was very poor—his letters were written for him and he was barely able to scrawl his signature—and his health, never robust, was precarious.

The importance of covering the Civil War had been recognized by men other than Brady.

Balaklava, looking seaward with the commandant's house in the foreground. By Roger Fenton.

Roger Fenton, the first "war photographer" who covered the war in the Crimea.

Ground over which the Light Brigade charged, showing the cannon balls covering the road like so many large boulders. By Roger Fenton.

Professor John W. Draper brought up the subject at a meeting of the American Photographic Society on June 10, 1861, and as president appointed a committee to discuss the matter with the Secretary of War.[20]

Draper's Committee, however, failed. They filed their suggestion with the War Department and it is not surprising to learn from Draper's report to the members that "little progress had been made in the matter owing to the extraordinary preoccupation of the department."

But Brady tried a different approach, that of personal friendship. In the winter of 1861 he traveled to Washington to try and get permission to have his staff pass through the lines.

When Brady arrived at his Washington gallery he discovered that Gardner already had prepared for war by outfitting the studio with a four-tube stereo camera to be used in making the expensive carte de visite.[21]

After consulting with Gardner and O'Sullivan, Brady saw his old friend General Winfield Scott. As he later explained to Gath Townsend: "In the days before the war it was a considerate thing to buy wild ducks at the steamboat crossing of the Susquehanna to take them to your choice friends and I often took Scott in New York his favorite ducks."

Scott, so swollen with dropsy he could not mount a horse, listened to Brady's plea. Then Scott told Brady a secret that only his aide Schuyler Hamilton knew; he was not to remain in command.

As Brady quoted Scott to Townsend in the *World* interview:

"Mr. Brady," he said, "no person but my aide, Schuyler Hamilton, knows what I am to say to you. General McDowell will succeed me tomorrow. You will have difficulty but he and Colonel Whipple are the persons for you to see."

Brady did not see McDowell then. Lincoln's inaugural took up most of his time, with Gardner making the preparations to cover the event. The first week in February Brady asked two of his best New York photographers, J. F. Coonley and C. M. Bernard, to come down from New York and assist Gardner and Tim O'Sullivan.

According to Bernard's wartime memoirs he and Coonley arrived in the capital at the same time as the Peace Commissioners. This would place them in Washington on February 4, 1861, when the commissioners, representing thirteen free states and seven border states, met at the request of the Virginia legislature. Brady was not one to miss a historic picture. He dispatched Bernard and Coonley to a former Presbyterian Church which had been taken over by the expanding Willard's Hotel, where the committee was to meet.

Coonley and Bernard fixed their Anthony and Company camera on the grim delegates and the quivering old man who sat directly beneath the faded oil painting of George Washington. It was the last picture taken of ex-President John Tyler of Virginia.

The drab inaugural was next on Gardner's and O'Sullivan's schedule. The security arrangements were strict and from the plates it appears that even Brady could not persuade Charles P. Stone, the brigadier general in charge of security, to relax his airtight arrangements.

Allan Pinkerton had just delivered Lincoln to Washington in a spectacular cloak-and-dagger fashion after the famous railroad detective had learned of a plot to kill the President-elect and Stone probably wasn't taking any chances—not even for Brady of Broadway.

Now war fever swept the country. Troops turned Washington into a war capital. There were parading baggy-pants Zouaves and even a regiment of mock Highlanders organized by the brother of Secretary Cameron. Willard's bar was packed every night, echoing with brave boasts of what they would do to Johnny Reb in this "six months war."

When Fort Sumter fell and Major Anderson became the hero of the hour, the demand for his picture was without precedent. Other military figures became popular and in the first months of the war the craze for collecting the tiny cardboard "calling cards" was felt in almost every American city, town, and village. The large galleries, including Brady's, began to produce the cards by assembly line production but the demand could not be met.

On Gardner's advice Brady entered into a

Harvest of Death, death of the Iron Brigade, the 24th Michigan Infantry, Gettysburg. By O'Sullivan.

contract with Anthony and Company. Brady delivered the negatives, the Anthonys produced the cards. All negatives then became the property of the Anthonys. For this Brady received about $4000 a year.

Now war was upon the land and the photographic coverage of the Civil War had begun. In later years Gardner contested Brady's claims that he alone had conceived the idea of compiling a photographic history of the Civil War, but circumstantial evidence gives credit to Brady.

What is clear is the feeling of resentment building up inside Gardner in those years. A precise, orderly minded Scot who respected a dollar, Gardner must have viewed with contempt the dapper, nonchalant Brady in his top hat, doeskin trousers, and the trail of lavender he left as he rushed off to Willard's to see his political friends. Some of Gardner's later actions also indicate he could be petty. There are a few hints of his querulousness and imperiousness. There is not a single memorable revelation of the man himself or his relationship to Brady.

O'Sullivan captured the human side of the war as well as the historic. Here Colonel Wood and his friends "mug" for O'Sullivan in camp at Culpeper, Virginia.

In the end they parted. Legend has Gardner leaving because Brady refused to allow any photographer to be given credit for an individual picture. It was probably not only credit but a number of things, including Gardner's resentment at Brady's seeming indifference toward the Washington gallery when a large percentage of the Washington gallery's profits was going to support the ornate New York City studio on Tenth Street.

O'Sullivan undoubtedly had a strong affection for the old photographer who had taught him so much from boyhood, but evidently stronger ties had developed between the intellectual Scot and the intelligent, sensitive Irish youth. O'Sullivan elected to go with Gardner.

There is evidence there was no outward bitterness. We find O'Sullivan taking Brady's picture at Gettysburg and Brady later writing a glowing recommendation for O'Sullivan years later when he was seeking a government post. I even suspect that Gardner was a sort of subcontractor to Brady and at times sold Brady second-best prints of what he, O'Sullivan, and his other photographers had taken. Unfortunately for historians, Brady wasn't entirely ethical, for when he resold them to *Harper's* or *Leslie's* they were credited "Photo by Brady."

Gardner, in partnership with his brother Jim, now set up his own gallery on the corner of Seventh and D Streets, N.W., called Gardner's Gallery, where in addition to photographs of all descriptions, from cartes de visite to "Ivory Types," he also sold books and stationery and "views of the war."

In July 1861 Brady began making his war

Brady's success in photographing the war was in part due to his friends in high places. Here, in his characteristic tall hat, he visits General Samuel Heintzelman at Arlington House, in Arlington, Virginia. Photo by Brady staff.

Early view of the Anthony Brothers, photographic suppliers who supplied Brady and O'Sullivan during the war and later during O'Sullivan's survey expeditions. Anthony photo.

Congressman Ely's picnic at Bull Run turned into an enforced six-month stay in a Confederate prison in Richmond. By Mathew Brady or an assistant.

Father Thomas H. Mooney, Roman Catholic chaplain attached in the 69th New York State Militia, saying Mass before Bull Run. Not long after, some of the soldiers photographed by Brady were among the regiment's 133 dead on the battlefield. Father Mooney was recalled by Archbishop John Hughes for several unconventional acts, most particularly the baptizing of one of the big guns mounted at Fort Corcoran, where the 69th was encamped, which he named the Hunter Gun and christened with holy water.

views in and around Washington. Regiments composed of three-month volunteers had arrived in April and May and were stationed at the various camps about the capital. Some of his first photographs were of soldiers of the Twelfth New York Regiment at Camp Anderson and the First Rhode Island Regiment at Camp Sprague and the Eighth New York Regiment.

On July 18 the half-blind Brady left Washington to photograph the first battle of the Civil War—Bull Run.

On that hot July day when Union troops, ambulances, and artillery caissons rumbled across Long Bridge into Virginia, Brady's strange wagon, soon to be called his famous "What-Is-It Wagon" bounced along the dusty roads to the good-natured jeers and hoots of the confident Federal troops.

It was a gay day, with scores accompanying the army, some like Congressman Ely and his ladies who brought picnic baskets "to see the Rebs beaten."

Bull Run took place, Stonewall Jackson received his immortal nickname, and Brady limped back into Washington, his plateholder filled with the first war views, including a poignant photograph of a Union trooper dead in the grass.

Brady, always history-conscious—and owning an acute sense of publicity values—stepped before his own camera and had his picture taken, still in his familiar linen duster and wearing the squat straw hat "like the French artists wear."

One of his most moving pictures of that first campaign was not of a battlefield. Somewhere along the way to First Manassas, Brady came upon the 69th New York Militia off to one side of the dusty road, attending a camp Mass, said by Father Thomas H. Mooney, the chaplain assigned to the 69th, then encamped at Fort Corcoran. Not too many hours after Brady took his picture, 133 members of the regiment would die on the Bull Run battlefield.

Brady was extremely active that summer. He photographed: Professor Thaddeus S. C. Lowe, who tried to make aerial observation of the enemy lines from his balloon; the foreign officers stationed at General Blenker's headquarters, where bands played and champagne was served; the cattle pastured on the banks of the Washington City canal for feeding the troops; sloops of war; colorful regiments like the Cossacks, Garibaldian Sepoys, and deserters from the French Foreign Legion.

But it was Brady's battlefield photographs of Bull Run that stirred Washington and demonstrated for all time to more cautious photographers how the camera could cover a war. Soon other photographers were raiding Brady's staff.

No one knows who accompanied Brady on his trip to the Bull Run battlefield. Ironically it might have been young O'Sullivan, who was still working for Brady—he doesn't appear as a war photographer for Gardner until five months later when we find him at Forts Walker and Beauregard in South Carolina. A few years after the war *Harper's Weekly* wrote an article about O'Sullivan's adventures in the Rockies and the author casually mentioned that "the Battle of Bull Run would have been photographed 'close-up' but for the fact that a shell from one of the Rebel field pieces took away the photographer's (O'Sullivan's) camera . . ."[22]

O'Sullivan was never a boastful man. If what he told the author of that magazine article in 1866 was true, can we not assume he was with Brady and had taken some of the first battlefield photographs of the Civil War for which Brady took credit?

Is it not unlikely that the half-blind Brady who now seldom operated a camera would venture alone in his bouncing wagon loaded with glass and chemicals to follow an army going off to battle?

But no matter who took the Bull Run battlefield photographs, they filled many photographers with the zeal to capture the Civil War on their glass plates.

The Anthonys, in addition to selling supplies, formed photographic teams, which included Thomas C. Roche, a former Brady man, who was taken on to make stereo views of the war.

But as soon as Brady lost one man he hired another. In the twenty years he had been in photography Brady had accumulated a sizable fortune, but as the months passed it began to dwindle. He was ordering enormous stocks of chemicals and glass from the Anthonys and his bills were astronomical. In the end they would inundate him . . .

Curiously, although the photographs taken by Brady, O'Sullivan, Gardner, and the other Civil War photographers certainly could have been considered militarily significant, photography as a weapon was not considered by either the military or naval organizations of the North or the South.

Pinpointing O'Sullivan's specific activities during the first year of the war is difficult. In his 1880 application for the job of chief photographer for the Treasury Department, O'Sullivan listed his war record as a "First Lieutenant attached to the staff of General E. L. Viele." However, a search of the Civil War military records, the pension lists, and New York militia rolls do not support his claim. O'Sullivan evidently was referring to his assignment as a civilian photographer attached to the Topographical Engineers for the purpose of copying maps and plans. The war views he took on his own were made with the knowledge he was risking his life or enduring hardships of weather, combat camps, and front lines, for photographs that may find their way into the principal news mediums of his day, such as *Leslie's* or *Harper's* or to be sold as "war views."

A study of O'Sullivan's earliest war views indicate the source of his "military service." In November 1861 he was following Captain Samuel F. DuPont's warships—which silenced Forts Walker and Beauregard—and General Thomas W. Sherman's troops—which went on to occupy first Port Royal and then the famous Sea Island of South Carolina.

O'Sullivan took a series of photographs of both forts in November and December 1861, then in March and April 1862 went on to Port Royal Island, Beaufort and Hilton Head. O'Sullivan was working for Gardner now serving as official photographer for the Army of the Potomac with the honorary rank as "captain" on General McClellan's staff.[23]

O'Sullivan, according to a Gardner letter written in later years, was "Superintendent of my map and field work." If his employer was "Captain," O'Sullivan probably had the honorary rank of "First Lieutenant," which he listed in his 1880 U. S. Treasury application. He also stated he was "discharged" at Hilton Head, South Carolina, in 1862—one of the last photographs he took of that campaign was Hilton Head, April 1862.

With O'Sullivan and Gardner now his competitors, Brady continued to add to his photographers "until I had men in all parts of the army like a rich newspaper," as he later claimed.

Although many photographers claimed in later years they were "official photographers" possibly only one man, Captain A. J. Russell, drew a salary as an official photographer for the United States Military Railroad. He maintained the government's only photographic laboratory during the Civil War. Russell was known to O'Sullivan and many times they met on the battlefields.

There were other semi-official photographers —men who submitted claims for the work they had done—such as George M. Barnard who accompanied Sherman's march to the sea and Sam F. C. Cooley, whose traveling darkroom was a familiar sight to O'Sullivan.

A study of the claims presented to the War Department for photographic work gives a cross section of the assignments handed out by the various departments. We find George L. Williams of St. Louis submitted claims for views he took of the construction of the Eads gunboats at Carondell; J. F. Sanders of New Haven for making scenes of the "Draft Rendezvous" in that city; R. G. Clary for his photographs of steam transports in New York Harbor.[24]

In addition to Gardner and Brady, who published their war views and gained national reputations, there were other photographers who independently operated behind the lines. Unlike Gardner and O'Sullivan they didn't even have a semi-official status.

Photographer's wagon for the Engineer's Department at Petersburg. This could be the darkroom for either Sam Cooley or Captain A. J. Russell, both attached to the Army of the Potomac as official photographers. Gardner and O'Sullivan had only semi-official status. Photo by O'Sullivan.

There were Davis Bachrach, founder of the famous Bachrach Photographers, Thomas Roche, A. Berger, who would take superb photographs of a war-weary Lincoln, and a little-known firm of Bergstrasser Brothers, who were primarily tintype operators but who also made war views. The New York *Tribune* of August 20, 1862, had this to say about the industrious brothers:

"Here for instance near General Burnside's headquarters at Fredericksburg, there are the combined establishments of two brothers from Pennsylvania, who rejoice in the wonderful name of Bergstrasser. They have followed the army for more than a year and have taken the Lord only knows how many thousand portraits. In one day since they came here, they took, in one of their galleries, 160 odd portraits at one dollar each (on which the net profit was probably ninety-five cents each). If anybody knows an easier and better way of making money than that, the public should know of it. The style of

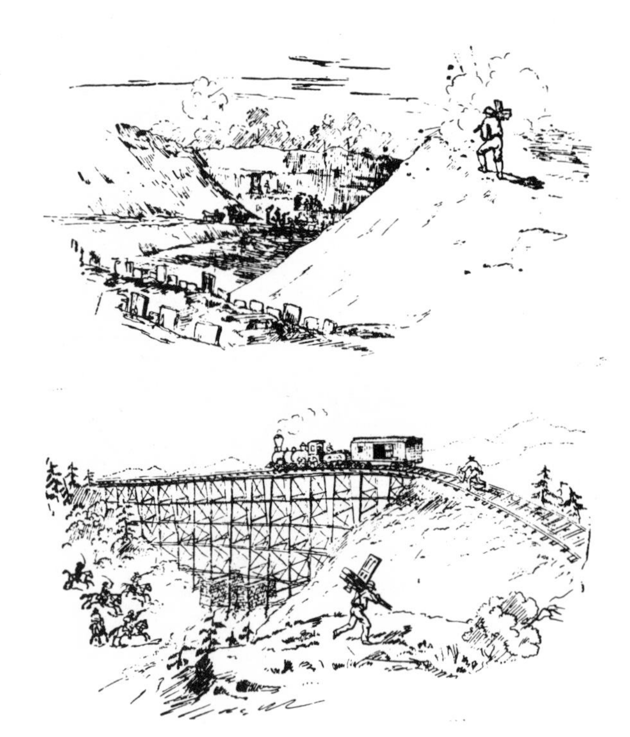

ABOVE, *Sketch of Roche, another of O'Sullivan's friends, and a former Brady man, dodging shells at Dutch Gap, from* Anthony's Photographic Bulletin, *1882.* BELOW, *Sketch in a photographer's trade journal showing O'Sullivan's friend George M. Barnard, former Brady photographer who accompanied Sherman on his March to the Sea. From* Anthony's Photographic Bulletin, *1882.*

portrait affected by these travelling-army-portrait-makers is that known to the profession as the melainotype or tintype."

The records show that photographers made money out of the war. If they couldn't sell their views to the news media such as *Harper's Weekly, Leslie's,* and the New York *Illustrated News,* they could easily find a market for them in the publishing firm of E. and H. T. Anthony in New York. Anthony and Company copied the views for their cartes de visite and duplicated them for sale in the thousands throughout the country.

Business records reveal Brady made about $60,000—roughly $12,000 a year from 1861–65—selling his war-view negatives to the Anthonys, but not many dollars stayed with him. He was always in debt to the Anthonys, probably because he insisted on turning back any profits to fulfill his dream of photographing the Civil War for history.

Not all photographers who covered the war were as idealistic. An examination of the Provost Marshal General's file, Army of the Potomac, reveals more than three hundred photographers received passes to enter the war areas, along with sutlers and tradesmen who wanted to sell oysters, roasted chestnuts, cigars, songbooks and soda water.

There is little doubt many left their homes, families, and photographic galleries, not for history but for money.

But no matter what their motives, idealistic or mercenary, the men who photographed the Civil War did so despite enormous difficulties. Getting to the scene of battle was only part of the task. For example, before O'Sullivan could capture one of his historic scenes he was first faced with the problem of obtaining fresh supplies, then transporting the tremendously heavy and fragile glass plates and his cumbersome equipment. Most of the photographers had wagons but few had money to invest in photographic vans and portable darkrooms. We believe that O'Sullivan had the latter.

But even after he overcame the problems of logistics and transportation, O'Sullivan faced others when he arrived at the scene: irritated or drunken officers, weather, foliage, herds of wandering livestock, or even a buzzing insect.

As Josephine Cobb, well-known Specialist in Iconography for the National Archives points out:

"Often in planning to photograph a significant war scene, the photographer found that no clear site could be discovered where their cameras could be set up, free of protruding branches or foliage. Occasionally a breath of wind, if not a stiff breeze, started up at the instance of exposure, thus ruining the chances of obtaining a picture. Horses, cows, and dogs, ambling back and forth within range of the camera, otherwise marked a failure for the photographer.

"Without the cooperation of the commanding officer of a military unit, group photographs and views of men at drill and on the march were not possible for the camera of the 1860s. Thus the photographer must be able to persuade the officer in command of the unit that photographs were desirable at the same time that other factors were favorable.

"Once the views were made, there were other possibilities of failure; a bug on the wet collodion before the plate had dried; drops of perspiration settling on the plate within the darkroom tent; floating leaves and other debris in the creek or stream where the photographer washed his plates after their development. And the fact that only in strong sunlight could outdoor views be made at all, made the work of the Civil War photographers arduous and uncertain . . ."[25]

There are eyewitnesses to such hardships pointed out by Miss Cobb. At least two of them described the hardships of Civil War photography for Francis Trevelyan Miller's researchers when he was gathering material for the text of his monumental *Photographic History of the Civil War*.[26] In 1912 George C. Rockwood recalled:

"First all the plain glass plates, in various sizes, usually 8 × 10, had to be carefully cleaned and carried in dust-proof boxes. When ready for action the plate was carefully coated with collodion which carried in its solution the 'excitants'—bromide and iodide of potassium, or ammonia, or cadmium. Collodion is made by the solution of gun-metal in about equal parts in sulphuric ether and 95-proof alcohol. The salts above mentioned are then added, making the collodion a vehicle for obtaining the sensitive surface on the glass plate. The coating of plates was a delicate operation even in the ordinary well-organized studio. After coating the plate with collodion and letting the ether and alcohol evaporate to just the right degree of 'stickiness,' it was lowered carefully into a deep 'bath holder' which contained a solution of nitrate of silver about 60 degrees for quick field work. This operation created the sensitive condition of the plate, and had to be done in total darkness except subdued yellow light. When properly coated (from three to five minutes) the plate was put into a 'slide' or 'holder' and exposed to the action of the light in the camera.

Home on wheels and workshop. Without their wagons, the Civil War photographers could not function. Photo by O'Sullivan.

When exposed, it was returned to the darkroom and developed."

Mr. Rockwood described Brady's What-Is-It Wagon as an "ordinary delivery wagon of the period, much like the butcher's cart of today" with a "strong step attached at the rear and below the level of the wagon floor. A door was put on at the back, carefully hung so as to be lightproof. The door came down over the step, which was boxed in at the sides, making it a sort of well within the body of the wagon rather than a true step.

"The work of coating or sensitizing the plates and that of developing them was done from this well, in which there was just room enough to work. As the operator stood there the collodion was within reach of his right hand, in a special receptacle. On his left also was the holder of one of the baths. The chief developing bath was in front, with the tanks of various liquids stored in front of it again, and the space between it and the floor filled with plates.

"With such a wagon on a larger scale, large enough for men to sleep in front of the darkroom part, the phenomenal pictures of Brady were made possible. Brady risked his life many a time in order not to separate from this cumbrous piece of impedimenta.

"On exceptional occasions in very cold weather the life of a wet plate might be extended to nearly an hour on either side of the exposure, the coating or the development side, but ordinarily the work had to be done within a few minutes, and every minute of delay resulted in loss of brilliancy and depth in the negative."

Mr. F. M. Rood, who went through the war in New York's Ninety-Third regiment, knew how delicate the operation was.

"The plate 'flowed' with collodion was dipped at once in a bath of nitrate of silver, in water also iodized, remained there in darkness three to five minutes; still in darkness, it was taken out, drained, put in the plateholder, exposed, and developed in the dark-tent at once. The time between flowing the collodion and developing should not exceed eight or ten minutes. The developer was sulphate of iron solution and acetic acid, after which came a slight washing and fixing (to remove the surplus silver) with solution of cyanide of potassium; and then a final washing, drying, and varnishing. The surface (wet or dry), unlike a dry plate, could not be touched."

During this period, numerous photographers moved through Brady's Washington gallery. Still every photograph had to be stamped "Photo by Brady" even though he did not actually operate the camera.

In the theater of war McDowell was replaced by George Brinton McClellan, whom Lincoln had summoned to Washington the day after the Battle of Bull Run. At thirty-four "Little Mac" took over the demoralized Federal Army, six days after it had fled from its first battlefield.

It was no army, as McClellan wrote his wife, "just a mere collection of regiments, cowering on the banks of the Potomac."

All that summer McClellan reviewed his troops, drilled, reconnoitered, drilled, and inspected, but never advanced. Lincoln grew uneasy, and more so in October when the Confederates repelled a small force at Ball's Bluff and planted a battery which commanded the Potomac.

The New Year turned, with the Confederates moved into winter quarters at Manassas.

Gardner, who all through his life seemed to go after projects rather than wait until they fell into his lap, received an assignment to copy maps and plans for the Army of the Potomac. He appointed O'Sullivan "field superintendent" and before the first spring rains O'Sullivan was with the troops.

This was the beginning of O'Sullivan's three years with the Army of the Potomac "as Civilian Photographer," as he described himself. He was on many major battlefields, from Second Manassas to Appomattox, and served under six generals. At Petersburg he dodged sharpshooters and artillery fire to get some of the unforgettable photographs of the war.

In March 1862, when McClellan indicated he was ready to move against him, General Joseph E. Johnson evacuated Manassas and Centreville and Union troops took possession of the works. O'Sullivan went along.

O'Sullivan traveled with the Army of the Potomac in a small carriage with canvas sides. It was not only his home but also his darkroom. It carried his plates, chemicals, and personal belongings. When the weather was clear he slept under it. In rain or snow, when no other quarters were available, he curled up in a blanket in the carriage's smelly darkness. Undoubtedly he ate with the noncommissioned mess. As an old soldier he knew the first man to be cultivated at a new camp was the mess sergeant. O'Sullivan probably did by taking his photograph; there is more than one mess staff among his plates.

In March he followed the army into Manassas and took a number of plates of the log huts the Confederates had erected and the raw Union troops now occupying them. Next was a combined operation that captured Fort Pulaski, guarding the mouth of the Savannah River and necessarily Savannah itself far up the river.

Pulaski was battered into submission and O'Sullivan moved into the fort with the first invaders. His photographs show the heavy Confederate guns overturned and the bomb-blasted brick casemate where the Confederates had their quarters, "a large kitchen, large table and benches and one large fireplace with a closet." There wasn't much left when the Union gunners finished. His pictures show the defenders

A lightweight photographer's wagon carrying a box labeled "Brady's." The man on the left is believed to be O'Sullivan. Photographer unknown.

employed some of the heavier guns as mortars by tilting them upward and using reduced powder charge.

The Union artillery general reported his guns had hurled more than one hundred pounds of shell into Pulaski. The damage they did to the old brick and mortar fort taught the Confederates a lesson. Pulaski demonstrated that a "yielding substance" had to be used against bombardments. Sand was selected and for the rest of the war sandbags and straw baskets filled with sand would be used in Sumter, Wagner, Vicksburg, and the other major Confederate works which underwent Union shelling. O'Sullivan's later photographs would show this.

In August, O'Sullivan joined General John Pope, whom Lincoln had brought out of the west to command the newly formed Army of Virginia, made up of troops from the Shenandoah and Rappahannock. The vain Pope, who had greeted his men with the grand observation that "I have come to you from out of the west where we have always seen the backs of our enemies," ordered General Banks to attack Stonewall Jackson's forces entrenched on Cedar Mountain.

The canvas-topped carriage of O'Sullivan's joined the line of march. On the morning of August 19, 1862, O'Sullivan perched his camera fifty feet or so from the bank of the Rappahannock to picture the Union artillery crossing to join the attack on Cedar Mountain. Later after General Samuel W. Crawford's brigade swept across the wheat field to smash the Confederate left, O'Sullivan hurried to record the scene where "our boys fought like heroes or devils; and although met by an enormous force of the enemy, they succeeded in driving him

Company C, 41st New York Infantry, after the Second Battle of Bull Run, 1862. By O'Sullivan.

back through one piece of woods into the open file, beyond. The fighting in this wood was most terrible; men fought bayonet to bayonet . . ."

The battle flowed back and forth, with the Confederates eventually claiming "undisputed possession of the field." After Pope issued his order for the army to retreat, troops and wagons moved out in the night with campfires left blazing to deceive the Confederates. As the first light broke, O'Sullivan again climbed the high bank to catch the wagons and weary troops recrossing the Rappahannock.

While O'Sullivan was photographing the retreating Federals, Lee sent Jackson around Pope hoping to destroy his supply lines. The lean, hard "foot cavalry" of Jackson swooped down on the Orange & Alexandria Railroad, ripping up the ties and destroying the stores. As far as an eye could see, as one trooper recalled, the ties were scattered, the rails twisted and the plain littered with boxes, barrels, cans, utensils, saddles, sabres, military equipment . . . most of the buildings were burned along with the tents.

When he heard the reports, O'Sullivan hurried on ahead. His photographs vividly show the results of Jackson's "visit" to the Yankee supply center.

Eleven days later O'Sullivan was in another battle, Second Bull Run. Lee had brought his army up by Thoroughfare Gap and McDowell, Longstreet, and Jackson joined in battle. The Union line broke under the charging gray line with the 2nd Virginia Cavalry leading the attack. It was a horrible disaster. The armies had barely left the field when O'Sullivan was scrambling down the muddy banks to photograph the small, brush-cluttered stream that would give the battle its name.

O'Sullivan seemed to be partial to New York regiments and one of his photographs was Company C of the 41st Infantry, taken shortly after the battle. Here are the hardened sergeants leaning forward, pipes clenched in their teeth, the officers with elaborate dignity and sabers casually to one side, the jack-booted colonel and his men sprawled about him . . . all desperately trying to appear like nonchalant veterans.

O'Sullivan's camera imprisoned them all . . .

In September, O'Sullivan met Alexander Gardner and James F. Gibson—later the manager of Brady's Washington studio—at Antietam and the three joined forces to capture on their glass plates the scenes of one of the bitterest battles of the war. Sharpsburg was battered by Union artillery when it was first believed the attractive little town was hiding Lee's troops. The shelling was indiscriminate but as the day wore on the Yankee gunners became more accurate and the shells found the Confederate positions.

The accuracy of the Federal gunners was due to a small group of Signal Corps officers atop a tower on Elk Mountain overlooking Antietam. Officers with telescopes were kept on the station "day and night, with but a few hours interval, from the commencement of the battle." A Richmond war correspondent glumly reported later that the Elk Mountain station had the Southern lines pinpointed:

"We could not make a maneuver in front or rear that was not instantly revealed to their keen lookouts . . ." he wrote.

O'Sullivan appeared at the station, simply a platform of crisscrossed logs, as Lieutenant Pierce, one of the two officers in charge of the station, was receiving a message from McClellan, presumably requesting information about some reported movement of Lee's troops. Pierce had a telescope to his eye reading off the message to Lieutenant Jerome, the co-commander of the station, when O'Sullivan snapped his first picture. Apparently after the answer had been sent, the officers and their three soldier senders, posed rather self-consciously for O'Sullivan.[27]

While O'Sullivan was at Elk Mountain, the Gardners moved up to Dunker Church and the cornfield fence where the Confederates had suffered badly. Later O'Sullivan joined an observer to photograph the Union's artillery bombardment, the deadliest since the war had started.

It is evident that O'Sullivan and the Gardners were present for the entire battle, which actually consisted of three major engagements: Hooker's attack on Jackson's lines in the East Woods, Hooker's advance on Lee's left which bent badly, and then the Confederate counterattack the next day. O'Sullivan's and Gardner's plates show the fury of the battle, but one wonders what glorious photographs they would have taken had their equipment been perfected to take movement: the Confederates running back through the cornfield with the Union troops cheering them "as if they had just won a ball game"; the Irish Brigade following General Israel B. Richardson as he cried, "Boys! Raise the colors and follow me!" Burnside's men gallantly storming across the narrow little Antietam bridge and the final attack by A. P. Hill, who fell on Burnside's exposed flank to save Lee's army . . .

It was a night of horror; dead and dying covered the fields. After a day's exposure in the hot sun the faces of the dead were black, the bodies swollen with the gas of decay. The stench was almost unbearable. Civilian volunteers aided the Medical Corps, who worked until they dropped. O'Sullivan's plates show the wounded lying under makeshift canvas covering in the open fields and in barns set up as temporary hospitals, and the makeshift graveyards.

On October 3 President Lincoln called on McClellan to urge him to advance on Richmond and Gardner was there to photograph the historic meeting.

A month later McClellan was ousted and Burnside took command of the Army of the Potomac.

The Signal Tower of Elk Mountain. The tower, on the south mountain range of the Blue Ridge, operated by Lieutenants Pierce and Jerome. When O'Sullivan appeared to take this photograph the signalman was just receiving a message from headquarters asking for the location of Confederate artillery.

The Gardners returned to Washington and O'Sullivan loaded up his wagon with chemicals and glass to join the Army of the Potomac now marching under Burnside's orders, to the Rappahannock opposite Fredericksburg.

When O'Sullivan made his camp on the shore he could see the attractive city across the river and the church steeples where Confederate lookouts watched the Union troop movements with glasses.

He could also see the stumps of the three bridges that the Confederates had blown, one opposite Falmouth, two opposite Fredericksburg. The army waited until the engineers came up and the 50th New York, one of O'Sullivan's favorites, were ordered to build five pontoon bridges.

The pontoons, which O'Sullivan photographed many times, were one of the most effective weapons of the war. As O'Sullivan joined the engineers he watched them break out the collapsible boats and start assembling them. The canvas, in one piece, was first smoothed on the ground. Then the bottom pieces of the wooden frame were put into place and the sides fitted into their holes. Next came the gunwales and the endpieces. The canvas was pulled up about the sides and made fast with rope running through eyeholes. The boat was then pushed into the water and allowed to soak to become watertight. Each boat was twenty feet long, five feet wide, and two and a half feet deep.

O'Sullivan was preparing to take a series of photographs of the engineers building the pontoon bridges when the rifles crashed across the river. Men screamed and fell. O'Sullivan calmly went on taking his pictures. When he had finished he gathered his equipment and left—probably ran—up the bank. The engineers were finally driven off and the artillery was called in to silence the sharpshooters.

By now a mist hung over the river and as the guns continued the bombardment, heavy powder smoke filled the air. By noon the barrage broke off. Men later recalled the sudden silence that fell over the river. Gradually the fog bank began lifting and the sun broke through, fiery as a molten cannon ball. Standing on the riverbank O'Sullivan could see the first glistening roofs of the city. Slowly the curtain of mist parted to reveal the bomb-wracked city. O'Sullivan carried his camera and plates to a peak on a small rise on a bank where he took a superb picture of the desolate city, its needle-pointed church steeples and the blackened bridge stumps. Later Burnside tried to take the city by storm only to lose the flower of his regiments before Marye's Heights. By nightfall the beaten army moved back across the bobbing pontoon bridges.

The following spring (1863) O'Sullivan found himself under another commander, Joseph Hooker, who had been wounded at Antietam. Hooker, a vain, boastful man, had many friends at the radical court and Lincoln selected him reluctantly.

"Don't call me 'Fighting Joe,'" he said. "It makes the public think I'm hotheaded . . ."

After Hooker arrived, headquarters became a gay place. Champagne flowed and the dashing young staff officers kept the parties going until the early hours to the disgust of the older officers.

O'Sullivan joined headquarters at Falmouth and took some pictures of the camp and Hooker's jack-booted young aides. There were old friends too at camp: Generals Meade and Sedgwick. After he photographed the generals and

General George G. Meade and his staff on the steps of Wallack's house, as photographed by O'Sullivan at Culpeper, Virginia, in September 1863.

their staffs, O'Sullivan went on to Hooker's supply camp at Aquia Creek Landing.

The winter was filled with alarms and excursions. Hooker kept harassing Lee by raids and forays; one by General George Stoneman left Confederate supply trains in ruins on the outskirts of Richmond. O'Sullivan stayed at the supply camp all winter. In the spring he returned to the banks of the Rappahannock where Jackson fell upon the exposed flanks of Howard's German troops to leave the regiment in a shambles. The Gardners were back in action with him now and they were later joined by Captain A. J. Russell. O'Sullivan left them for what appeared to be a major action at Chancellorsville up the river, but to the dismay of his officers Hooker ordered his troops back to their defensive positions. O'Sullivan, however, managed to get some plates, once hurrying to the river's edge to snap truce parties exchanging the wounded.

Jackson's attack had been successful but costly for the Confederates. He was shot by mistake and died on the tenth. Sedgwick stormed Marye's Heights to Chancellorsville, the newest Federal disaster, which would prompt Lincoln to sadly shake his head and wonder, "My God, what will the country say?"

Hooker was still in command but the Army of the Potomac was discontented. Stoneman had been relieved of his command for his now-famous raid, and Sedgwick bitterly complained Hooker was trying to make him a scapegoat. There were no more champagne parties that winter and rumors had a new commander appearing with the spring showers . . .

It was spring and Lee was on the move. Federal outposts in the Shenandoah crumbled under his cavalry attacks and soon the roads were packed with wagons and refugees who kept moving until they were clear into Pennsylvania. The tidal wave of gray troops was like a Biblical locust plague across the countryside. Houses, cattle, household goods, horses vanished. Only devastation was left.

In Falmouth the troops heard the rumors but continued to polish their rifles and mend their gear. There was no new commander, only Hooker. The Army of the Potomac was now lean. The twenty thousand short-term troops had gone home and the losses from Chancellorsville had not been made by any levies. Hooker now had less than seventy thousand troops on hand.

Stonewall Jackson as a young man, from an original Daguerreotype.

The hot June days were filled with news of Lee's advance. In Washington clerks eyed the mounds of records they had to burn. Lincoln studied the messages and asked for one hundred and ten thousand militia from Ohio, Maryland, and Virginia.

On June 28 Hooker resigned in a huff over the question of keeping troops at Harper's Ferry and Meade was appointed Commander of the Army of the Potomac.

It was a terrible move. The Army of the Potomac was on the verge of a clash with a fast-moving aggressive enemy and a new commander had been appointed, in what was obviously an act of sheer desperation. The lean hard troopers packed their gear and set out behind their new commander who felt that he should follow Lee and force him to turn and fight.

The Army left Falmouth in a forced march

Rocks could not save him from the fury of the onslaught. The Devil's Den at Gettysburg. By O'Sullivan.

and with them was O'Sullivan, who more than ever in the next few days would be history's eyes . . .

The long columns wound their way north, the troops bedecked by flowers tossed at them by laughing farm girls. Even the veterans boasted of the miles they had put behind them, sometimes thirty a day, and the militia that struggled alongside them at the crossroads were greeted with hoots and good-natured jeers. The days were pleasant, the countryside peaceful. War was far in the distance.

When they rested O'Sullivan went among them, taking their pictures in front of stacked arms, or sprawled about their campfires eating, or just grinning into the camera. On the morning of July 1, A. P. Hill's skirmishers came riding over the ridge near Willoughby Run, a small brook which crossed the graveled pike that ran toward Cashtown, a little village half a dozen miles to the west of a town named Gettysburg.

A corporal and three troopers of the 9th New York Cavalry met them and exchanged shots—the first of Gettysburg.

Millions of words of vivid, moving prose have been written about Gettysburg in the century after those bloody three days, but it is O'Sullivan's photographs which make it all real.

In O'Sullivan's photographs nothing stands between the viewer and the battlefield. The scene is there, undistorted by myth, legend, and the repetition of false tradition: the stiffened corpses robbed of their boots and accounterments by a tattered army defeated that day but determined to fight again and again; the quiet fields where the dead lay, hidden by the tasseled wheat; the rocks and underbrush of Devil's Den; the sleepy crossroads village; the curious, phlegmatic gravediggers; the sad and solitary wooden markers.

There is little doubt O'Sullivan was near the action for the three days. He was on the field the morning of the second, the third, and the fourth day. He and his camera were on the field as the battle moved on: on the wheat field, the field where the Iron Brigade was almost wiped out; Little Round Top, where Lieutenant Hazlett's guns never cooled; Devil's Den, where the sharpshooters hid among the rocks and picked off General Weed as he bent down to catch Hazlett's dying words; then Torstle's Barn where the Confederate batteries found their mark to leave light Union artillery battery scattered about, men and horses dead in the thin rain.

O'Sullivan was also at Meade's headquarters, "a tiny farm house, sixteen by twenty," where the Rebel gunners zeroed in and the screaming shells killed all the staff's horses which had been hitched to the fence and the trees.

Brady appeared on the second day and so did Alexander Gardner. For Gardner the trip was unexpected. He had received word in Washington that the battle was nearing the seminary at Emmitsburg, Maryland, where his fifteen-year-old son, Lawrence, was a student. Gardner hurried to the school—not forgetting his camera, plates, and chemicals—which at the time was held by the Confederates. He was taken prisoner at Farmer's Inn in Emmitsburg. Apparently he was able to convince the Rebels he wasn't a spy for he was allowed to return to Union lines with his son. Before he left, he photographed the Inn where he had been held prisoner and many of the areas on the battlefield almost immediately after the Confederates had withdrawn.

But it was O'Sullivan's superb photographs which stunned the country. *Harper's* devoted its August 27th edition to telling the story of

Farmer's Inn, where Alexander Gardner was captured by the Rebels, July 5, 1863. After questioning he was released. By Alexander Gardner.

the battle and ironically gave Brady credit for some of O'Sullivan's photographs. A brief story in the magazine said:

"Mr. Brady, the photographer, to whose industry and energy we are indebted for many of the most reliable war pictures, has been to the Gettysburg battlefield and executed a number of photographs of what he saw there . . ."[28]

How did this happen? Why did O'Sullivan's brilliant work get into *Harper's* with credit to Brady? No one knows the answer. It may be that Gardner sold some of his prints to Brady, as he did many times, and Brady returned to New York and gave them to *Harper's*—with his byline.

Certainly there was no ill feeling between Brady and young Tim. Before he left the battlefield, O'Sullivan took the old master's picture in Devil's Den and on the field where General Reynolds had fallen . . .

One of the last pictures O'Sullivan took of that bloody place was the Gettysburg Cemetery, quiet on a hilltop just south of the town. There was a wooden sign by the gatepost announcing that the town would impose a five-dollar fine on anyone who discharged a firearm within the cemetery limits . . .

The Army of the Potomac moved slowly, reluctantly, after Lee, but even pressure from Halleck and Lincoln could not force Meade to engage the Confederates in another major battle. Lincoln shook his head and said, "We had only to stretch forth our hands and they were ours . . ."

O'Sullivan stayed with the Army until it moved into winter quarters. As always there were the small log huts chinked with mud, the drinking, gambling, horse races, cockfights, and greased pig and pole contests. There were brief skirmishes, one at Culpeper Court House where Custer struck a glancing blow at Lee's rear guard before Meade finally made his camp at Culpeper.

O'Sullivan made several photographs of the area, including the courthouse and the tenting grounds near the graceful old church. Then the couriers arrived with the news Lee might be

Alexander Gardner's portrait of Lincoln in 1863.

swinging about in a mad rush to come between Meade and Washington. To prevent this Meade moved back as far as the Old Bull Run battlefield at Centreville. Then Lee dropped all pretense and swung back southward, burning the railroads and bridges in his path.

The engineers were ordered out ahead of the army and O'Sullivan went along photographing the bridge builders at Catlett's Station, Virginia, and along the Rappahannock as they rebuilt the spans, assembled the inevitable pontoon bridges and laid the planked roadbeds across them. Before the first snow there were a few more raids, particularly Kilpatrick's bold attempt to free the prisoners in Richmond, but that was all. The weary Army settled at last in winter quarters. O'Sullivan seems to have been on the move, going from camp to camp, photographing the works, the men, the officers, and even the bands and cockfights. His photographs give a vivid picture of the rough, even bawdy winter quarters of the now professional Army of the Potomac, at Brandy Station, Culpeper, along the Rappahannock and at Germantown. Undoubtedly he wintered at Brandy Station where the Telegraphic and Photographic Headquarters were located. The huts there were made of logs with canvas roofs. There was a washline, a broken chair, a woodpile and a broken swing. One wonders how they spent the long gray days.

In the spring the opening skirmishes began for what was to be one of the most fatal years of the war. Sherman organized his expedition against the railhead at Meridian, Mississippi, Banks started his Red River march, Sherman was given command in the west, and Grant took Vicksburg and was placed in full command of the Union Army.

O'Sullivan was now serving under his sixth general . . .

On May 5, O'Sullivan and his camera were at the Wilderness where men fought in a virgin forest of oak and pine, choked with underbrush. It was so thick the troops moved in single line, the powder smoke so heavy, that men stumbled blindly into enemy lines. Two days later O'Sullivan was with Grant, moving toward Spotsylvania, where on May 8, Grant and Lee faced each other again. One of the last pictures O'Sullivan made before the battle began was of his old friend General Sedgwick, who liked to describe himself as "practical as distinguished from the theoretical soldier," standing on the steps of a house surrounded by his staff. A short time later Sedgwick would be killed, as he told a soldier dodging Rebel bullets not to worry, "they could not shoot an elephant at that distance." The words had just fallen from his lips when he fell, killed by a sharpshooter.

O'Sullivan moved in as the initial battle was ending. His photographs of the dead Confederates were the most poignant he had taken since Gettysburg. During the five days that both armies rested O'Sullivan searched for Grant. He found him and his staff holding a "council of war" at Massaponax Church, Virginia, and that morning O'Sullivan took a series of photographs that rank among the best taken in the war. Grant had ordered his staff to remove the pews from the tiny church and arrange them in a semicircle for his generals. With an eye of getting the complete dramatic picture instead of the usual individuals, O'Sullivan climbed into the church belfry and took a series of pictures as the restless Grant conferred with his officers and made his decisions.[29]

After the conference, O'Sullivan moved out with Sheridan on his "raid of ten thousand sabres." On the North Anna River the Federals captured the Beaver Dam Station and destroyed a million and a half Confederate rations. Here they met Jeb Stuart's cavaliers but Sheridan neatly sidestepped him, crossing the North Anna River by Ground Squirrel Bridge and moving on toward Richmond until he reached Yellow Tavern, six miles from the Confederate capital. O'Sullivan appears to have been keeping up with the raiders. He caught his old friends the 50th Engineers building another pontoon bridge across the North Anna and even photographed a group swimming below the railroad bridge they had just constructed. In an action at Yellow Tavern, Jeb Stuart was wounded and removed to Richmond, where he later died. For the Confederates it was a loss comparable to Jackson.

Sheridan attempted to take the works around Richmond while the flamboyant Custer led his troopers across the first line to return with a bag of prisoners. Lee, meanwhile, fell back gradually from the area around the North Anna until he was completely covering Richmond.

After the Sheridan action it appeared O'Sullivan rested; where or how we don't know. The meager vital statistics tell us he was married. Did he return to New York to see his sweetheart, or his father who apparently was very close to him?

With O'Sullivan away from camp, Alexander Gardner took over and it was his camera that was present at Kennesaw Mountain where Sherman's troopers stormed the tangled wood slopes and rifle pits in the face of heavy rifle and artillery fire. When the last shot had been fired, the first movement of Sherman's drive against Atlanta was over.

In November Sherman began his famous march to the sea while Grant lay siege to Petersburg. George M. Barnard accompanied Sherman; O'Sullivan remained with his Army of the Potomac.

General William T. Sherman as photographed by Brady or an assistant.

Petersburg, south of Richmond, was the central point for five railroads linking the South Carolinas with Virginia. Its capture could force the evacuation of the Confederate capital. From the beginning it was a fight to the finish with neither side asking quarter.

O'Sullivan was with Grant from the beginning of the siege to the end. Curiously, although we know he was working for Gardner we find him with Brady at a Union battery. O'Sullivan took the old man's picture as the guns slammed and Rebel shells whined overhead. Forty-seven years later the commander of the battery recalled the picture when the editors of the *Photographic History of the Civil War* asked him to identify it. Again tradition won out and Brady got all the credit. As Lieutenant James A. Gardner wrote:

"I am, even at this late day, able to pick out and recognize a very large number of the members of our battery, as shown in this photograph. Our battery (familiarly known as Cooper's Battery) belonged to the Fifth Corps, then commanded by Gen. G. K. Warren.

Brady under fire at Petersburg. Another photograph by Tim O'Sullivan at Petersburg. In this shot much has been made of Brady, who is standing by the battery, but what of O'Sullivan, who is taking his photograph?

"Our corps arrived in front of Petersburg on June 17, 1864, was put into position on the evening of that day, and engaged the Confederate batteries on their line near the Avery house. The enemy at that time was commanded by General Beauregard. That night the enemy fell back to their third line, which then occupied the ridge which you see to the right and front, along where you will notice the chimney (the houses had been burnt down). On the night of the 18th we threw up the lunettes in front of our guns. This position was occupied by us until possibly about the 23rd or 24th of June, when we were taken further to the left. The position shown in the picture is about six hundred and fifty yards in front, and to the right of the Avery house, and at or near this point was built a permanent fort or battery, which was used continuously during the entire siege of Petersburg.

"While occupying this position, Mr. Brady took the photographs, copies of which you have sent me. The photographs were taken in the forenoon of June 21, 1864. I know myself, merely from the position that I occupied at that time, as gunner. After that, I served as sergeant, first sergeant, and first lieutenant, holding the latter position at the close of the war. All the officers shown in this picture are dead.

"The movement in which we were engaged was the advance of the Army of the Potomac upon Petersburg, being the beginning of operations in front of that city. On June 18th the division of the Confederates which was opposite us was that of Gen. Bushrod R. Johnson; but as the Army of Northern Virginia, under General Lee, began arriving on the evening of June 18th, it would be impossible for me to say who occupied the enemy's lines after that. The enemy's position, which was along on the ridge to the front, in the picture, where you see the chimney, afterward became the main line of the Union Army. Our lines were advanced to that point, and at or about where you see the chimney standing, Fort Morton of the Union line was constructed, and a little farther to the right was Fort Stedman, on the same ridge; and about where the battery now stands, as shown in the picture, was a small fort or works erected, known as Battery Seventeen.

"When engaged in action, our men exhibited the same coolness that is shown in the picture

One of a series of Grant portraits taken by Brady or one of his Washington staff in 1864. The portraits were discovered in a New York State barn wrapped in a Washington newspaper of the 1870s.

A weary Grant in a Brady portrait, taken shortly after his promotion to the rank of Lieutenant General and General-in-Chief of the Army.

—that is, while loading our guns. If the enemy is engaging us, as soon as each gun is loaded the cannoneers drop to the ground and protect themselves as best they can, except the gunners and the officers, who are expected to be always on the lookout. The gunners are the corporals who sight and direct the firing of the guns.

"In the photograph you will notice a person (in civilian's clothes). This is Mr. Brady or his assistant, but I think it Mr. Brady himself.

"It is now almost forty-seven years since the photographs were taken, yet I am able to designate at least fifteen persons of our battery, and point them out. I should have said that Mr. Brady took picture No. 1 from a point a little to the left, and front, of our battery; and the second one was taken a little to the rear, and left, of the battery. Petersburg lay immediately over the ridge in the front, right over past the man whom you see sitting there so leisurely on the earthworks thrown up."

Lieutenant Gardner's memory was probably faulty so many years later. One of the photographs taken at the time included Brady. Gardner didn't explain how the old master could have taken his own picture with the gun battery.

Another gunner that day recalled how the cannoneers and the corporals who sighted the pieces had to lay flat behind the guns for protection from Rebel balls and fragments and it was "expected" that officers would stand "upright." O'Sullivan was almost naked in his exposure to the Confederate guns as he took his pictures.

While the Confederates probed all that winter for weakness in Grant's twenty-five-mile long line (his parallels extended for ninety miles), O'Sullivan searched for pictures. He was at Fort Hell or Damnation, which was constantly under the fire of sharpshooters in the city. Veterans later recalled it was worth a man's life to expose an inch of his cap.

O'Sullivan's superb photographs clearly show the trenches, tunnels, and parapets of sand-filled baskets along with the barrels and gabions used to lengthen the chimneys needed for heating the underground huts. The distance between the lines at the point where O'Sullivan took the pictures was 1500 feet.

The crew of the Dictator, the massive mortar that haunted the city, also knew O'Sullivan.

Fort Hell—Fort Sedgwick. The veterans used the barrels as smokestacks and chinked the log walls with mud. By O'Sullivan.

The 13-inch 200-pound gun was mounted on a flatcar reinforced with railroad iron. It ran down the track of the Petersburg and City Point Railroad to a point where a curve made it easy to change the direction of fire. The recoil from the monstrous gun, which used fourteen pounds of powder for each shot, lifted the mortar two feet each time it was fired and shifted the flatcar a dozen feet on the rail.

The usual full charge was twenty pounds of powder.

Fort Sedgwick, or Hell or Damnation, as the troops called it, was vividly photographed by O'Sullivan. It was not an elaborate engineering feat but it had to be sturdy to withstand the pounding of the Confederate guns in Fort Malone. After the war the sturdy works began to disappear under another siege—the wood-hungry natives and the rain. Within two years not a trace was left of the tunnels, trenches, and parapets of sand-filled baskets which O'Sullivan's camera had captured for history.

O'Sullivan stayed with the Army of the Potomac all that winter as the mortars made the winter-gray sky pulse with sound and the twig-snapping noise of the rifles usually meant that one of the boys in Fort Hell had been testing the Rebs with a hat on a stick, or a man had carelessly stuck his head over the sand basket parapets.

For the troops in Fort Hell or Damnation the winter was dreadful but for the Confederates it was agonizing. As one Confederate recalled, it was a lucky day when his sergeant drew seven pounds of rancid bacon—three days' rations—for his fifteen men, and how the men, "like dogs for a bone," waited for their portions.

Despite the rain, snow, and freezing nights

the Federals managed to break the monotony of the long months with the usual cockfighting, horse racing, gambling, "Commissary whiskey and broken noses."

In January of 1865 O'Sullivan joined his second combined operation with Fort Fisher, the mightiest fortress of the Confederacy, as the target. The fort, on the North Carolina coast near Wilmington, guarded the port longest open to blockade-runners. It was a powerful bastion with heavy timbers, heaped fifteen to twenty-five feet thick with sand sodded with marsh grass. The fort was equipped with heavy fire-power, seacoast guns, ten-inch Columbiads and six-inch rifles on wooden carriages, lined up wheel to wheel.

Sixty vessels, including five ironclads, arrived before the fort on the morning of December 20, under Admiral Porter. It was the largest force ever assembled under one command in the history of the United States Navy. After a futile attempt to breach the walls by sending in a flaming powder boat on the night of the twenty-third, the fleet moved into line and began a tremendous bombardment. The frigid air shook with the roars of twenty-five nine-inch guns. On Christmas morning the bombardment was resumed with a landing party moving ashore under the fire cover. The raiders were repelled, but a few weeks later, on January 13, Fisher fell.

O'Sullivan went ashore soon after the Stars and Bars fluttered downward. His photographs, starting from the wide strip of beach where the landing parties hit, up along the traverses—earthworks built perpendicular to the main work in order to limit the destructive area of shells—and then into the bomb-blasted fort, are an awesome record of what Fisher endured that Christmastime.

Spring found O'Sullivan back with the Army of the Potomac before Petersburg. In the Union lines the smell of victory was in the air, strong and fresh as the morning April breeze that made the flag look like hammered tin. The Army was restless, ready to move out. In Fort Malone the Confederate gunners were still sending over shells but with a measured reluctance.

A damaged, yet still vivid photograph of the destruction of a Confederate gun position at Fort Fisher, 1865. By O'Sullivan.

"You must not be surprised if calamity befalls us," Lee warned Richmond.

While the army waited impatiently, O'Sullivan moved about the camps with his camera, probably exchanging gossip with the foot soldiers probably cursing their wooden-headed officers, as soldiers have always done in the spring since Caesar's legions. Everywhere, except before Richmond, the Confederate armies were retreating, their lines crumbling. The fall of Fisher now meant complete strangulation of the thin lifeline of blockade-runners. On March 26 Sheridan reached City Point and Grant was ready to move against Petersburg, the final campaign of the war.

On April 1 the reinforced cavalry and infantry struck Lee's extended lines at Petersburg. The Confederates fought desperately but the lines broke.

"It happened as I told them in Richmond it would happen," Lee said. "The line has been stretched until it is broken."

Fort Gregg, the Confederate salient nearest the Federal lines, sullenly surrendered under a massive artillery barrage followed by a savage saber-swinging cavalry charge with the horses leaping the parapets. Petersburg was no longer tenable. On April 2 Lee's forces began drawing to the north side of the Appomattox River, destroying the bridges as they retreated. In the early hours, the first points of the Federals cautiously entered Petersburg and at four o'clock

With the fall of Petersburg, Richmond could no longer be held. Retreating Confederate troops burned their stores to keep them from falling into Federal hands. Soon large sections of the city went up in flames. Here is a view by Gardner of the burned area taken soon after the holocaust.

the flag of the 1st Michigan Sharpshooters was hoisted above the graceful old courthouse with its dignified statue of Justice.

The bridges leading into the city were gone but the veteran engineers had the pontoons assembled and the roadbeds down in short order. It must have seemed an old story to Tim O'Sullivan as he drove his traveling darkroom across the swaying planks; Fredericksburg, North Anna River, and the stark chimneys of Jericho Mill; Pulaski, then Fisher last month, with the overturned seacoast guns, and long before that the gray dawn of the second day at Gettysburg . . .

He was among the first in the city, probably swapping comments or jokes with the other Gardner photographer, John Reekie, as he set up his camera to catch the first canvas-covered wagon train rumbling down the muddy street just off the river, while the women and the children huddled under umbrellas watched silently and fearfully.

In Petersburg, O'Sullivan took numerous pictures of the occupying army and the city itself. Then he was on the move again with the determined Grant, who wanted to end it once and for all. It was still raining, the roads were hub-deep, but the Army of the Potomac swept down, never stopping, cheering Grant when he appeared and boasting how far they had come this day.

It was a week of hounds and hare with Lee's army melting every hour. On April 8 Custer, looking like a "circus man" with his red bandanna and tilted soft black hat, captured trains of supplies. There was no way left to run and now the horns of the hunters were loud in the ears of the gallant Lee. It had to be surrender.

Wilmer McLean's beautiful old farmhouse was selected as the meeting place. In the parlor on the left Lee wore the spanking new gray uniform buttoned to the throat, a handsome sword and sash. Grant, the unbuttoned dark blue blouse, the top boots with the trousers inside—spattered with mud.

There were a few minutes of small talk, then

It fell to Custer, shown here on the left with General Alfred Pleasonton, and his cavalry to harass the hard-pressed Confederate supply lines. This may be an O'Sullivan photograph.

The McLean family posed for O'Sullivan on the steps of their home soon after the terms of surrender were signed.

The war was over and the nation celebrated. Here is a photograph by Brady or one of his assistants, of the grand review of the Federal troops in Washington, D.C.

Brady's portrait of Lee taken in Richmond, shortly after the surrender. Posed with Lee is his son G. W. C. Lee and Lieutenant Colonel Walter H. Taylor.

the terms. Lee accepted. It was over in a few minutes. Lee went out on the porch and signaled for his mount. While the horse was being bridled he gazed sadly in the direction of the valley where lay the tattered remnants of his army and his cause. Three times he hit the palm of his left hand with his right . . . he rode off with Grant on the porch saluting him . . .

It was the greatest moment for a photographer but Brady, Gardner, and O'Sullivan did not arrive in time. Apparently O'Sullivan was the only one to reach McLean's but the principals in one of the most moving moments in our history were gone.

Evidently O'Sullivan arrived at the McLean house a short time after the signing because one of his negatives show eight troopers, rifles neatly stacked, still on guard.

It would be fascinating to know what O'Sullivan's thoughts were when he learned what he had missed; they were probably agonizing. He did the next best thing and grouped the McLean family on the steps of the house to take several poses, then snapped the soldiers. Alexander Gardner meanwhile had hurried on to Richmond to make a memorable series of that devastated city.

But it was Brady, the old master who took the honors. He hurried to Richmond to persuade Lee to pose with his son, G. W. C. Lee and Lieutenant Colonel Walter H. Taylor of his staff, in the basement below the porch of Lee's Franklin Street home in Richmond.

As the story goes, Brady told a servant he wanted to see Lee, whom he had known since the Mexican War. Lee came to the front porch and said, "It is utterly impossible, Mr. Brady. How can I sit for a photograph with the eyes of the world upon me today?"

Brady then sought out Mrs. Lee and Exchange Agent Robert Ould, whom he knew very well and they persuaded the general to pose. Despite his dimming eyes and fumbling hands the old master took superb and unforgettable photographs. A century later the grief and the fallen glory is still visible in Lee's tired eyes.

1861–1862: THE OPENING ROUNDS

Among O'Sullivan's first war photos are these taken during the initial Federal campaign against the Confederate coastal fortifications in 1861. Fort Walker in South Carolina was one of the first to fall.

A Federal siege train at Hilton Head, South Carolina, late 1861.

With the coming of spring in 1862 the Confederates left the winter quarters at Manassas and as soon as the Federal troo moved in, so did O'Sullivan with his camera.

The eastern range of the Confederate winter defenses at Manassas, early in 1862.

ederal encampment at Blackburn's Ford near Bull Run in Virginia, July 4, 1862.

·deral military railroad siding at the supply depot of Manassas, July . The former Confederate fortifications are in rear.

The headquarters of General Irvin McDowell at Manassas in July 1862. This was formerly used by General P. G. T. Beauregard.

The Union hospital at Manassas in July 1862. At this time the former Confederate stronghold was a Union supply base.

Fredericksburg, Virginia, one of the oldest cities in the United States. O'Sullivan's view shows the waterfront of the city which extended about a mile with brick and stone buildings lining the right-angle streets. The Confederates had left only the blackened piers of the three bridges leading into the city when O'Sullivan peared, probably accompanying the 50th New York Engineers built the pontoon bridges under heavy sniper fire.

ery in action at Fredericksburg. O'Sullivan took this photograph while under fire of Confederate guns.

eral McDowell's engineers constructing a bridge across the north fork of the Rappahannock in the vicinity of Fauquier Sulphur Springs, ginia, in August 1862.

The important railroad depot at Warrenton, Virginia, in August 1862.

The road leading out of Warrenton, Virginia, with t courthouse in the distance, taken by O'Sullivan in Aug 1862.

Refugees hamper any moving army and the "counterbands"—Negro slaves of the Civil War—were commonplace to the Union Army. In August 1862, when Pope's troops were moving in on Cedar Mountain to attack Johnson's entrenched forces, O'Sullivan's camera caught a bewildered uprooted family, its few house goods piled high on the ox cart, as they crossed the Rappahan River.

n the summer 1862, Union engineers were working day nd night to repair the bridges and railroads demolished y the Confederates to stall an advance on Richmond. 'Sullivan's camera caught the engineers constructing a ridge over the Rappahannock River near Sulphur Springs. ngineer Herman Haupt recalled General McDowell told m he never heard "sweeter music than the click of hamers when we were working all night near his headquarrs."

In August 1862, Tim O'Sullivan's canvas-topped wagon joined Pope's forces moving in on Cedar Mountain. On August 19 he perched his camera on the bank to photograph the newly constructed bridge spanning the Rappahannock River.

ion artillery fording a tributary of the Rappahannock, August 9, 2, the day of the Cedar Mountain battle, also known as the le of Slaughter Mountain. Edwin Forbes, the artist, described the Union lines battling "bayonet to bayonet" . . . with Stonewall's Brigade.

The famous wheat field at Cedar Mountain across which Brigadier General Samuel W. Crawford's Brigade charged against the Confederate left. Crawford lost a big part of his command on this field.

A panoramic view of the Cedar Mountain battlefield, Augu 9, 1862. This is the center of the battlefield with the Unic camps in the foreground.

A Union supply wagon on a street in Culpeper, Virgi 1862. Most of the troops stationed in Culpeper found it be almost a deserted village with the twenty stores do little or no business and few of the fifteen hundred reside seen on the streets.

Culpeper Court House, 1862. This scene shows the courthouse whose steeple was familiar to most Union troops, and a group of Confederate prisoners, taken at the battle of Cedar Mountain, on the balcony.

A typical street scene in Culpeper, Virginia, where M made his headquarters. While he found the area to be "best country in Virginia we have yet been in" his tro found it a dismally deserted village and with "no res male or female seen on the highways."

diamond-stack engine and a freight train at Culpeper, Virginia, in 1862. This Orange & Alexandria Railroad were targets of Jack-'s foot cavalry in the summer of 1862.

engineers all knew O'Sullivan. In August 1862, on the banks .e Hazel River, a tributary of the Rappahannock, O'Sullivan's camera caught at least one of the crew of engineers swimming after having just finished repairing the wooden bridge.

While O'Sullivan was photographing Pope's army retreating across the Rappahannock, he heard of Jackson's raid on the Orange & Alexandria Railroad, at Manassas Junction, Virginia. O'Sullivan hurried to Pope's supply depot, where his camera recorded th damaged cars, ripped and twisted rails.

Catlett's Station, Virginia, an important Union supply depot, photographed by O'Sullivan in August 1862, showing the Union troops a supply train.

ailroad stock destroyed by Jackson's troops.

lepairing the Orange & Alexandria Railroad at Catlett's Station after Jackson's Raid, August 27, 1862.

A new bridge across the Bull Run built by McDowell's engineers in August 1862 before the Second Battle of Bull Run. A ph tographer's wagon, possibly O'Sullivan's, is at left.

Bull Run Bridge, sometime after the Second Battle of Bull Run, Saturday, August 30, 1862. One of Jackson's troopers vividly remembered how the Union lines advanced "as regular as if they were on drill" only to break under the deadly fire a few yards from the Co federate lines. Three times the Union lines advanced until Pop entire front fell back in retreat.

1863: TO GETTYSBURG

Lutheran Theological Seminary.

Evacuation of Aquia Creek, June 1863. This photograph was taken by O'Sullivan a few hours before the Army of the Potomac started to use it and Belle Plain, seven miles below this point, as bases for retreat. Barges, steamboats, and small craft were used in ferrying the army across. The supplies and stores were burned wh hysteria gripped the countryside after the rumor spread that t Confederates had outflanked the army and were moving on Was ington.

Provost Marshal's Office, Aquia Creek, where soldiers of the Civil War's Army of the Potomac showed their passes for leave.

Fairfax Court House, June 1863, the village of Fairfax. Courthouse eighteen miles from Washington where, as O'Sullivan's caption describe it, "the best homes were burned, churches were converted into hospital then into stables, while the venerable courthouse was stripped of its wooc work." In 1864 loopholes for riflemen were cut in the sides of the builc ing. Hooker and McClellan both used it as their headquarters. Th Bull Run battlefield was ten miles distant.

ɔnfederate prisoners in Fairfax, captured in the battle of Aldie · General Pleasonton's troops. The majority, according to O'Sulli- n, were dressed in "shabby gray pants and jackets and worn felt hats worn by Rebel cavalry." The battle took place at the foot of the upper end of Bull Run range of hills in Loudoun County in the village of Aldie.

stle Murray, near Auburn, Virginia. There was no depot on the arrenton Railroad and it was three miles to the nearest station, the physician's home called Murray's Castle was taken over Union staffs under General Pleasonton in 1863. O'Sullivan alled how at night the green lamps of the camp "shone mysteri- ly upon the field and the field band of the Sixth U. S. Cavalry de the stone walls ring to martial music."

Pontoon bridges across the Rappahannock. The bridges used by the First and Sixth Corps when they crossed one and a half miles below Fredericksburg to join the battle.

Battery D, Second U. S. Artillery, in action, Fredericksburg, Virginia, June 1863. When the Sixth Corps crossed the Rappahannock, Battery D took up its position in the field near the Marshfield house. O'Sullivan made this photograph just as the cry rang out, "Cannoneer to your posts!" The second order was for O'Sullivan to move unless he wanted to be a casualty. The line to the rear beyo the battery is the Veteran Vermont Brigade. This battery had se so much action, O'Sullivan noted, there was no room for all its bat standards.

Falmouth, Virginia, April 1863. Men and wagons of the Engineer Corps ambulance train.

Gettysburg, Pennsylvania, the "capital of Adams county, on the turnpik to Philadelphia and Pittsburgh." Along this road the Federals retreated tc ward Cemetery Hill on the late afternoon of July 1, only a few hours befor O'Sullivan arrived on the battlefield.

dge at Hanover Junction burned by Confederates before the battle of Gettysburg.

tysburg, Pennsylvania, July 1863. Headquarters of General George G. Meade during the battle of Gettysburg.

"The field where General Reynolds fell." One of a series of O'Sullivan's unforgettable Civil War pictures. This is the Federal dead, July 1, 1863. All the way from McPherson's Woods back to Cemetery Hill lay the Union soldiers, who had contested every f of thv retreat until nightfall.

Trossell's house, Gettysburg, where General Sickles had his headquarters. For a time the fighting swirled about this spot and when O'Sullivan arrived there were thousands of dead horses and n about the house.

erior of the breastworks on Round Top, Gettysburg, was occupied the Fifth and Sixth Corps on the second day.

The Slaughter Pen, at the foot of Little Round Top, Gettysburg.

e Slaughter Pen. At the time O'Sullivan appeared with his camera, the woods at the front of the ridge were full of Union and Con- lerate dead.

Gettysburg, Pennsylvania, 1863. Little Round Top. Battlefield of Gettysburg. The man on the left is probably Brady.

Gettysburg, Pennsylvania, July 1863. Dead Confederate sharpshooter.

he gateway to the Gettysburg Cemetery, the scene of some of e bitterest fighting, especially on the afternoon of the third day hen about one hundred and twenty pieces of Confederate arlery, along with 18,000 troops appeared to be headed for the nter of General Hancock's line. There was fierce, close fighting in which the Federals took "between thirty and forty colors and 4500 prisoners." O'Sullivan snapped this photograph as the gravediggers were arriving with more corpses. It was on this spot that O'Sullivan noted a sign warning anyone "discharging firearms in this vicinity will be fined."

cene of Pickett's charge, Gettysburg.

Gettysburg, Pennsylvania, July 1863. John L. Burns, the "old hero of Gettysburg," with gun and crutches.

Gettysburg, Pennsylvania, August 1863. General hospital.

Confederates captured at Gettysburg.

Culpeper, Virginia, September 1863. General George G. Meade's headquarters, Wallack's house.

tysburg, Pennsylvania, August 1863. U. S. Sanitary Commission.

gons and horses attached to repair department, in charge of Captain Pierce, Army of the Potomac, September 1863.

Catlett's Station, Virginia, vicinity. Building railroad bridge across Cedar Run. (Destroyed by Confederates when they fell back before Army of the Potomac under General Meade, October 1863.)

Culpeper Court House, November 1863, with a Union camp on the edge of town.

Camp in the woods, Culpeper, Virginia, vicinity, November 1863.

FORTS AND FORTIFICATIONS

Phillips Island, South Carolina, November 1861. Fort Beauregard.

Fort Pulaski, Georgia, April 1862. The "Jeff Davis" gun.

Fort Pulaski, April 1862. View of guns: "Jefferson Davis," "Beauregard," and "Stephens."

Fort Pulaski, April 1862. The "Beauregard" gun.

rt Pulaski, April 1862. The breach.

Fort Pulaski, April 1862. Distant view showing the effect of the fire from assault batteries.

Ruins of Fort Pulaski, captured in April 1862.

Fort Pulaski, April 1862. Interior view of front parapet.

im O'Sullivan was one of the first photographers inside Fort Fisher, North arolina, when it fell. Here he photographed the first three traverses of the eat fort. O'Sullivan accompanied the Navy operation which gathered at ampton Roads, December 24, 1864, under Rear Admiral Porter. The task rce consisted of 67 vessels, 5 ironclads, and a reserve force of 192 vessels nder General Ben Butler. Butler's troops tried to take the fort but failed. later attempt succeeded.

The Pulpit at Fort Fisher which was finally taken by 8000 men under Major General A. H. Terry, on January 13–14, after the task force's devastating fire. At 3 P.M. the first troops landed with O'Sullivan not far behind. At 10 P.M. the fort fell, 140 sailors and marines landed to capture 75 guns and 1900 prisoners. The Rebels, in their retreat, then blew up four companion forts to prevent their being captured by the Union attackers.

w of first traverse, northwest end showing entrance to fort.

Fort Fisher, North Carolina, January 1865. Interior view of traverse and magazine on the land front.

Fort Fisher, January 1865. Interior view, showing traverse with dismounted gun.

Interior view. English Armstrong gun.

Fort Fisher, January 1865. Interior view, with heavy gu broken by naval bombardment.

1864: THE BEGINNING OF THE END

Winter quarters at Rappahannock Station, Virginia, March, 1864. Officers' huts, 50th New York Engineers.

Sutler's hut and the stockade of the 50th New York Engineers at Rappahannock Station, Virginia, March 1864.

Colonel George H. Sharpe's quarters. Headquarters, Army of the Potomac. Bull ring in the distance. Brandy Station, April 1864.

Headquarters of the Army of the Potomac, Brady Station, Virginia, 1864, General Rufus Ingalls' quarters.

pontoon boat at Brandy Station. As O'Sullivan pointed out, en the boats were used permanently as a bridge a "box lantern" uld be placed at each end of the bridge. When night fell the try at one end of the bridge would slam the door of his box three times "which would signal to the sentry at the other end that the bridge would soon be occupied by a team or a train." O'Sullivan's wagon is in the rear.

In May 1864 the armies of Grant and Lee girded for battle. For the balance of the year the armies were seldom out of contact with each other as Grant maneuvered his forces toward Richmond. Here are the ruins of the bridge at Germanna Ford with the Unio[n] forces in the background.

Lee contested the Union drive toward Richmond at both the Wilderness and Spotsylvania. Here is a view of a Union artillery unit taken from Beverly house looking toward Spotsylvania Court Hou[se] on May 19, 1864.

Burial of soldier by Mrs. Alsop's house, near which Ewell's Corps attacked the Federal right on May 19, 1864.

Confederate dead laid out for burial at Mrs. Alsop's Pine Forest, May 20, 1864, three miles from Spotsylvania Court House, Virginia.

Confederate soldier of Ewell's Corps killed in the attack of May 19, 1864.

After Spotsylvania, Grant shifted his troops toward the east to get around Lee. Here are the Federal pontoon bridges across the Pam key, with wagons. Hanovertown Ferry, Virginia, May 1864.

"Departed Greatness," a relic of the past century found by O'Sullivan near Guiney's Station, Virginia, May 21, 1864.

Massaponax Church, Virginia, May 21, 1864. View of the church whi was the temporary headquarters of General Ulysses S. Grant, surround by soldiers.

t's Council of War at Massaponax Church, Virginia, May 21, . General Grant is leaning over the shoulder of General Meade, ining a map which had just been finished by the topographi- ngineers. This is the first of a series of three photographs taken by O'Sullivan from the church's steeple. O'Sullivan's elevation made the series much more dramatic than static shots taken on ground level. O'Sullivan etched the sequence of the plates in the lefthand side of the plate, No. 730.

Grant, after having examined the map, returned to his seat to write a dispatch.

rant, having written the dispatch, waits a reply. He is sitting with Meade, Assistant Secretary of War Dana and their staff officers.

Chesterfield Bridge on the North Anna, also known as Telegraph Road to Richmond. The 93rd of New York carried its colors to the center of the bridge under Hancock in May 1864. According to the 10th Massachusetts they rushed across this bridge "one piece at a time, to present a little target."

Quarles' Mill, North Anna, from the south side. General Headquarters, Army of the Potomac, in the distance, May 1864.

Ruins of a bridge across the North Anna River. The framework was still smoking when O'Sullivan arrived with the Union troops at the end of Sheridan's ride to the outskirts of Richmond.

Quarles' Mill, Virginia, May 1864. View on North Anna at Quarles' Mill, looking upstream.

Quarles' Mill, May 1864. View of log bridge at Quarles' Mill, North Anna, where a portion of the 5th Corps under General Warren had to cross and carry the enemy's line of works on the crest of the hill.

A lull in the battle. Federal soldiers bathing, North Anna River. Ruins of Richmond & Frederick Railroad bridge in the distance.

A moment of rest on the pontoon bridge on North Anna, below railroad bridge where a portion of the 2nd Corps under General Hancock crossed, May 23, 1864.

Bethel Church, Virginia, May 23, 1864. View of the church, temporary headquarters of General Ambrose E. Burnside.

Grave of General J. E. B. Stuart in Hollywood Cemetery, with temporary marker. Richmond, Virginia, 1865.

View of the mills and the pontoon bridge from the south bank. Jericho Mills, May 24, 1864.

'he Rappahannock River front at Port Royal, Virginia, May 30, 1864.

rant's troops at Charles City Court House, Virginia, June 13, 1864.

Charles City Court House, June 13, 1864.

Harbor, Virginia, June 4, 1864.

Belle Plain, Virginia, 1864. Army wagons and transports at the lower landing.

Hampton Roads, Virginia, December 1864. Fleet of Fort Fisher expedition.

THE HUMAN ELEMENT

The halt. Captain Harry Page, later Lieutenant Colonel Page and Chief Quartermaster of the Cavalry Corps, was photographed by O'Sullivan resting after he had finished selecting a camp position. Here he is "waiting for the wagons" so he can supervise the pitching of the tents and the parking of the wagons in the wagon park.

Officers and noncommissioned officers of Company D, 93rd New York Infantry. Bealeton, Virginia, August 1863.

Winter quarters of Colonel Howard, Chief Quartermaster, 3rd Army Corps, Brandy Station, Virginia, February 1864.

General Isaac J. Stevens, Beaufort, South Carolina, March 1862.

Band of the 114th Pennsylvania Infantry (Zouaves). Brandy Station, Virginia, April 1864.

Provost Marshal General Marsena R. Patrick and staff. Culpeper, Virginia, September 1863.

General Post Office, Army of the Potomac.

Troopers of Company D, 3rd Pennsylvania Cavalry (2nd Division, Cavalry Corps), Brandy Station, Virginia, March 1864.

fighting at General Orlando B. Wilcox's Headquarters before Petersburg. 1864.

Architecture. When the engineers, sitting out the siege of urg, had some idle time they would construct fancy signal and "distinguished quarters for their officers." Here is one taken by O'Sullivan just outside the Petersburg line with hedges and archways, "pretty enough to have the officers send for their wives."

General Judson Kilpatrick of the 3rd Division, Cavalry Corps, Culpeper, Virginia, September 1863.

idence of John Minor Botts. Culpeper, Virginia, vicinity, September 1863.

m Corps of 61st New York Infantry. Falmouth, Virginia, March 1863.

Guard mount, Headquarters, Army of the Potomac. A Zouave company, 114th, Third Corps, in winter headquarters āt Culpeper

Culpeper, Virginia, November 1863. Negro contrabands at leisure.

Mountain, Virginia, August 1862. Family group before the house in which General Charles S. Winder died.

May 20, 1862. The staff of General Fitz-John Porter; Lieutenants William G. Jones and George A. Custer reclining. The Peninsula, Virginia.

Negroes preparing cotton for the gin on Smith's plantation, Port Royal Island, South Carolina, 1862.

Sutler's bombproof "Fruit and Oyster House," Petersburg, Virginia.

Camp of Company B, 93rd New York Infantry, Bealeton, Virginia, August 1863.

The Army of the Potomac's Wagon Park at Brandy Station. This is one of O'Sullivan's superb Civil War photographs, taken despite the constant threat of insects that could mar the wet plates, hundreds of uneasy horses, drunken teamsters, and impatient officers. This collection of men and wagons consisted of carpenters, saddle makers, field shops, wheelwrights who shod thousands of mules every d repaired from 400 to 500 wagons and ambulances, repaired or ma officers' desks, furniture, and post office appliances. In this pict O'Sullivan caught 240 wagons, a part of the Army of the Potoma 6000 wagons which in "the line of march" stretched 60 miles

The Telegraph Construction Corps of the Army of the Potomac, putting up wire "on the march." The corps consisted of 150 men, wire, horses, and wagons. From 1861–62 "common wire" was used, late in 1862 "flexible wire" was substituted which could be used in reels. Later, insulated wire was used. When poles were not available, wire was strung along fences and hedges. The cavalry patrols made the local residents responsible for the condition of the wire.

e Commissary Department "which was nothing less than a large cery establishment." Here, as O'Sullivan noted, the clerks sold fee, tea, molasses, beef, salt pork, potatoes, rice, and flour. The r before this view was taken, large quantities of food were sold to families of Confederate soldiers, "some walking twenty miles to buy their food." The prices were all "marked below the wholesale price."

General Alfred Pleasonton's headquarters. General Judson Kilpatrick is at right. Auburn, Virginia, October 1863.

A field repair shop in the Ninth Army Corps "before Petersburg." In the far right are the "stock" where the shoeing of the mules took place. The animals were lead in "by a peck of oats," then suspended by a belly band in mid-air. Four men grabbed the mal's hoofs, fastened them with leather thongs, and nailed on shoes. The tent fly is used as a wall for the blacksmith's forg

General Robert O. Tyler and staff of the Artillery Reserve. Culpeper, Virginia, September 1863.

Discussing the probabilities of the next advance.

Group in front of post office tent at Army of the Potomac Headquarters. Falmouth, Virginia, April 1863.

Military telegraph operator. Headquarters, Army of the Potomac, August 1864.

Brandy Station, Virginia, April 1864. General Rufus Ingalls on horseback.

Falmouth, Virginia, April 1863. Group at A.A.G. office.

Alfred R. Maud, special artist of Harper's Weekly *sketching the battlefield of Gettysburg.*

Camp of the 18th Pennsylvania Cavalry, near Brandy Station, March 1864.

Lord (William) Abinger and officers at Headquarters, Army of the Potomac, Falmouth, Virginia, April 1863.

Headquarters of the Army of the Potomac, at Brandy Station, just before the opening of the Battle of the Wilderness. The large tent is General Meade's. Tents of the staff usually formed a circle in front of the commanding general's with the camp enclosed by brush fences and having plank footwalks.

A breakfast party at Headquarters, Army of the Potomac, April 1864.

Drum Corps, 93rd New York Infantry, near Germantown, Virginia, August 1863.

iew of Mill's plantation. Port Royal Island, South Carolina.

leton, Virginia, August 1863. Group at tent and wagon of the New York Herald.

1865: PETERSBURG

Courthouse in Petersburg, Virginia, April 1865.

Charles City Court House, twenty-five miles southeast of Richmond, the scene of severe cavalry fighting in 1862, 1863, 1864. General Meade's troops sacked it going from Cold Harbor to Petersburg in 1864.

High Bridge Crossing of the Appomattox showing the High Bridge of the South Side Railway from Petersburg to Lynchburg. The bridge was 128 feet high, 2400 feet long. On the morning of April 7, 1865, the Second Corps, Army of the Potomac, captured the bridge after Confederates tried to burn it and the road below. The engineers replaced the burned parts with a three-span section.

The historic Appomattox Station on the railroad between Petersburg and Lynchburg, Virginia, 96 miles to Petersburg and 3 miles to Appomattox Court House. O'Sullivan arrived here when the last train carrying supplies to Lee was captured by a fast-moving Union striking force on April 8, 1865. The Confederates, mostly young boys and old men unarmed, were transferring supplies when the Union cavalry struck.

Farmville, Virginia, vicinity, April 1865. High Bridge of the South Side Railroad across the Appomattox.

etersburg Gas Works and the pile of bricks which once was the famous eighty-foot Petersburg Gas Works smokestack. The Federal batter-es used it to take aim and it finally collapsed.

view on Appomattox River near Campbell's Bridge, Peters-g. In O'Sullivan's view on the righthand side is the Merchants' Manufacturing Company Cotton Mills, which employed 150 to 200 employees, the sawmills and the company mills.

Johnson's Mill, Petersburg, Virginia, known as Furts' Mill, below Bolling Dam on the Appomattox River near Campbell's Bridge. Built in 1773, this was one of several large flour mills in the vicinity, that produced three hundred barrels daily for the Confederate Army.

The Poplar Grove Church built at Petersburg by the 50th New York Volunteers Engineers, March 5, 1865. Toward the end of the war it was proposed to move it to Central Park, New York City, but this never came about.

Headquarters, 50th New York Engineers. Petersburg, Virginia, November 1864.

fficers' quarters and church at Poplar Grove Camp of the 50th New York Engineers.

ullivan's view of the interior of Fort Stedman, "one of the ad-ced positions in Petersburg." O'Sullivan's photograph, which ost appeared to be a lithograph, shows the parapet of earth supported by trunks of trees placed horizontally, reinforced by gabions and fascines and topped by sandbags. On the extreme left are the officers' quarters. May 1865.

Bombproof, Fort Stedman.

Interior of Fort Stedman; bombproof in foreground.

Railroad battery, Petersburg, Virginia.

Railroad gun and crew, Petersburg, Virginia.

This is Fort Sedgwick, called "Fort Hell" by the Union troops. Each bomb shelter in this picture had its own fireplace-barrel for a chimney and the hut was plastered with mud. As O'Sullivan's caption said: "Here only the reckless would dare expose the slightest part of a person."

Fort Stedman earthworks in front of Petersburg.

Bombproof shelters on the lines before Petersburg, 1864. This was the advanced point where it was said: "It was certain death to look over the side of the trench." The dugouts here were under a constant, almost hourly bombardment from Confederate guns only a few thousand yards distant.

Fort Sedgwick with its wall of sand-filled gabions and chevaux de frise. *A few years after the war, rain had completely wiped out all evidence of the rough, sturdy, dirt and sand fort.*

Execution of William Johnson for attempted rape, June 20, 1864, Petersburg, Virginia.

ıbt near Dunn's house in outer line of Confederate fortifications which General William F. Smith captured June 14, 1864. Peters- Virginia.

or view of the Confederate line at the Gracie salient, opposite Haskell where a dam made a small lake and where the troops were constantly cold and wet with no dry wood to burn during the time of their stay.

Captain James Cooper's Battery, 1st Pennsylvania Light Artillery, before Petersburg, June 21, 1864. Brady is the man with his hands in his pockets behind the lead gun. O'Sullivan who took the picture, was warned by the gun captain to get his camera and portable darkroom out of the line of fire.

Captured Confederate encampment, Petersburg, Virginia, June 1864.

Rebel works in front of Petersburg, 1864, captured by the 18th Corps under General Smith, June 25, 1864.

Soldiers' quarters, Petersburg, Virginia, August 1864.

The McLean house at Appomattox Court House where O'Sullivan and all the other Civil War photographers missed history's most moving photograph: the surrender of Lee to Grant.

O'Sullivan, when he arrived, photographed the soldiers in front of the mansion and also the McLean family on the porch. He noted that the apple tree in the rear where Grant met Lee was "carr away by souvenir hunters, with not even the roots remaining as mentos." Curiously, the McLeans, photographed by O'Sullivan, had a house on the First Bull Run battlefield, "but left it to sec relief from visitation of an army."

Appomattox Court House, Virginia, April 1865. Civilians in front of the hotel.

Appomattox Court House, April 1865. Federal soldiers.

4

THE KING EXPEDITION: 1867–69

"There is, in the entire region of the (Shoshone) Falls such wildness of beauty, that a feeling pervades the mind almost unconsciously that you are if not the first white man who has ever tried the trail, certainly one of the very few who has ventured this far . . ."

John Sampson, quoting Tim O'Sullivan in the article, "Photographs from the High Rockies," *Harper's New Monthly,* September 1869

A dismal drizzle of rain was falling as twilight came to Washington on one of the greatest days in the life of Clarence King, scientist, aristocrat, friend of the powerful, intimate of the influential. At the age of twenty-five he was to lead an expedition into the wilderness of the West to tell Congress, the Army, the nation what lay out there between the front range of the Rockies and the eastern slope of the Sierra Nevadas. Was it true there were diamond fields? And what about the great coal deposits? Was the land so fertile you could thrust down a cane and it would sprout branches and leaves? Could it take to the plow? Could it be sold, cultivated?

King was ready to take to the field to answer these questions. He knew he had been lucky to get this appointment. Only that afternoon Secretary of War Stanton had handed him his commission as chief of the United States Geological Exploration of the Fortieth Parallel and told him quietly:

"Now, Mr. King, the sooner you get out of Washington the better. You are too young to be seen about town with this appointment in your pocket. There are four Major Generals who want your place."

The hearing that afternoon before the Congressional Committee had been brief. At one point Ben Butler had asked in amazement:

"Do you mean to say there will be no regular army officers, no West Pointers in this thing?"

"No one," King had replied.

Butler leaned forward, his crooked eye fixed on King.

"And you are all civilians?"

"Yes, sir."

Butler leaned back and roared, "Then by God it shall go through."[30]

Ben Butler still remembered those "ramrods," as he called the West Pointers, from the Civil War days.

There was something of a mystery how this young, handsome scientist received such an important commission from Congress. Henry Adams, his close friend and admirer, years later wrote it wouldn't do to investigate what "happy accident" brought about the appointment, but in those early years success and adulation from the powerful and influential were commonplace with Clarence King.[31]

King makes a strange companion for Tim O'Sullivan, but for three years they would live together, the quiet-spoken photographer who

Clarence King in camp, dressed as a dude. Whenever a visitor appeared, even a lonely miner, King would insist that he dress for dinner. By O'Sullivan.

Exploring Expedition to the Rocky Mountains.

Among the passengers to California this week was a party of young men on an important surveying expedition to a section of the Rocky Mountains and the great basin westward. The work is to be prosecuted subject to an order of Congress, under the direction of the Secretary of War, acting through Gen. HUMPHREYS, the Chief of the United States Engineers. The party consists of the following named gentlemen: Chief, CLARENCE R. KING; Topographical Assistants, James Gardner, H. Custer, Frederick A. Clarke; Geological Assistants, Jas. D. Hague, Arnold Hague, Sam'l F. Emmons; Botanist, W. W. Bailey; Zoologist, Robert Ridgway; Photographer, T. H. O'Sullivan. Of the Chief, Mr. KING, we learn that he is a young graduate of the Sheffield Scientific School of Yale College. The Hartford *Courant* says he has recently been attached to the California Geological Survey, and without detracting from the distinctions of other scientific men he may be said to have reached already greater eminence than any one in this country, for he has been, if we are rightly informed, on the highest mountain peak that has been attained within the limits of the United States. When the party reaches California, they will be joined by a detachment of 20 or 30 cavalrymen, detailed to act as their escort to the remote mountainous and desert region to which they are going. The section to be surveyed is a belt of land about 100 miles wide, near the 40th perallel of latitude, between the 120th and 105th degrees of longitude, or in other words, from Virginia City to Denver City, a stretch of 800 or 900 miles in length. This strip includes the proposed route of the Central Pacific Railroad, on which the work is progressing so rapidly, and it is the object of the Government to ascertain all the characteristics of the region which is thus to be traversed. The "lay of the land" is first to be ascertained, and an accurate map prepared, which will exhibit the hills, valleys and plains, in all their variety and configuration. Then search is to be made for coal, the discovery of which may be of more value to the railroad than a gold mine; and for water, which in the desert track between the Sierra Nevada and the Rocky Mountains proper, is not always to be found when wanted. The minerals, the flora and the fauna of the country, and its agricultural capacity, are likewise to be studied and reported on. In fact, all the work of nature in that wild and unknown region is to be scanned by shrewd and highly-educated observers. Three years are to be expended in the survey, and perhaps three years more will be occupied in working up the result; but preliminary reports will be sent on from time to time, embodying all the discoveries of immediate practical interest. The outfit of the party is excellent, including all the variety of mathematical and geodetic instruments which will be required for the nicest measurements, barometers, sextants, levels, compasses, etc., of the best construction, besides the necessary articles for the comfort and protection of the travelers. The corps speaks gratefully of the hearty interest which has been manifested by Gen. HUMPHREYS, of the War Department, in providing this apparatus, and of the value of Gen. A. B. EATON'S coöperation in originally promoting the appropriation for the survey.

The small article on page eight of the New York Times *announcing the departure from New York City of King's party for Panama and the West Coast, May 8, 1867. Tim O'Sullivan is listed as "Photographer."*

smelled of mules and chemicals and the handsome young scientist who insisted on dressing for dinner while the wolves were howling in the hills and the sagebrush was bouncing against the tents like great balls of twine.

O'Sullivan would follow King for three years across the Western mountains and plains, sharing many adventures and incredible hardships. Years later when both would know adversity and sickness they would recall each other with much warmth and affection.

King's appointment was an attempt to answer the much-asked question of what sort of land was out there in the deep West. There had been expeditions such as the Pacific Railroad Surveys, sent out by Jefferson Davis, in 1851 to find out if there was a possible railroad route. To a large part of the country after the Civil War the West was a wonderland made up of half-truths, myths, and legends, a land that rumbled and fired great geysers of hot water high into the air, of vast coal fields that had been burning since time began, of weird tribes that lived in apartments carved into the sides of sheer cliffs. And added were the usual tales, of diamond mines, mountains of gold, and Coronado's legend of the Gilded Man.

Four great geographical and geological surveys would be conducted by the government from 1867 to 1879 until the United States Geographical Survey—still in existence—took over. Two would be conducted by King and Lieutenant George Montague Wheeler. King led the United States Geological Exploration of the Fortieth Parallel, and Wheeler led the United States Geographical Survey West of the One Hundredth Meridian. The objects of all the surveys were topography, geology, and the natural sciences. O'Sullivan would be on both the King and Wheeler surveys. It was his pictures, obtained after great hardships and physical risks that helped to change the deep West from wonderland to reality.[32]

The surveys and the men who led them are virtually unknown today except to specialists and scholars, but the development of our country owes much to them. Bernard De Voto wrote:

"These men built up the knowledge of which establishes the habits of millions of Americans, shapes their businesses and in fact makes possible the way they live."[33]

The King Expedition, the first and probably the most important, was led by a fascinating man who had an extraordinary talent to attract men from every facet of life: cowboys and buffalo hunters, clerks and hotel men, railroad builders, clergymen, poets, statesmen, artists, and writers. As one of his friends said of King years after his death:

"To use the well-worn phrase of Dickens he was the delight of the nobility and the gentry."

King was an aristocrat "to the fiber" although he came from an impoverished family.

"If there were any graceful and inoffensive ways of doing it," he once wrote to his friend, the famous geologist James D. Hague, "I wish it could be intimated in my life and engraved on my tombstone that I am to the last fibre aristocratic in belief, that I think the only fine thing to do with the masses is to govern and educate them into some semblance of their superiors." Then he tried to soften this snobbery with, "This is ticklish ground and you may not like to impair my presidential chances by frivolities of this kind."[34]

King knew and was liked and admired by the influential, the powerful, and the wealthy. He liked fine wines and good food, art, poetry, and conversation. He was particularly fascinated with dark women—he married a Negress. Although King made several fortunes in mining he died in debt. One of his creditors was John Hay, Secretary of State, to whom he owed $44,800.

King was impetuous and generous. John La Farge pictured him as a man who would plunge into his old studio on Tenth Street, "filled with buffalo skins and Indian lances and come up with a Turner or a Millet from among the trunks and give them to a friend . . . for it pleased him to have others enjoy what he had not the time and the place for . . ."[35]

And Henry Adams in a paper read before the Century Club said: "We would at any time and always have left the agreeable men in Eu-

Clarence King, in the Mintah Mountains. By O'Sullivan.

rope or America to go with him. We were his slaves and he was good to us. He was the ideal companion of our lives."[36]

King, at the time he knew O'Sullivan, was a slender, blue-eyed man with close-cropped hair, and a "brilliant and charming creature" as William Dean Howells called him. When Howells met him, King had just come back from a California expedition and had written a series of articles for *Atlantic* which had been put into a book called *Mountaineering in the Sierra Nevada*—an immediate best seller.[37]

The year before, after graduating with the first class of Yale's Sheffield School of Science, he had made a journey west with his friend and classmate James Terry Gardner. Their object was to cross the plains on horseback. They reached St. Joe, the great jumping-off place, and when word came that the buffalo grass was green an immigrant train moved out with King and Gardner riding beside the wagons.

They followed the old Frémont Trail, up the North Platte and the Humboldt Rivers into Nevada. They stayed in Virginia City—where a few years later King and O'Sullivan would winter and where Tim would make a series of historic photographs—but a fire gutted their clapboard boardinghouse, destroying all their possessions. King went to work in a quartz mine. Three weeks later he and Gardner were crossing the Sierra Nevada. In August 1863, about the time the country was weeping over O'Sullivan's moving pictures of Gettysburg, King met Professor William H. Brewer of Yale, then second in command of the Geographical Survey of California. The famous Josiah Dwight Whitney was his chief.

King and Gardner were aboard a Sacramento River steamboat on the way to San Francisco to see Whitney to apply for jobs when they accidentally met Brewer on deck. Brewer took an immediate liking to King who, he thought, "looked much younger than his twenty-two years."

When Brewer asked King what had brought him to California the young scientist replied Mount Shasta had been the "magnet" that had drawn him to California and he was determined to climb it.

Later Brewer and King scaled Mount Shasta and Lassen Peak "with King quoting Ruskin and Robertson's sermons" as they inched up the sheer cliffs.

This trip is said to have been the turning point in King's life. As they descended the mountain, they discussed a stream which King said could be glacial.

"At the time, I said I doubted this," Brewer recalled. "Later when King discovered the glaciers on Shasta he proved he had been correct that morning. However, it was at this point that I talked to King much about the value of photography in geographical surveys. I had taken a fancy to stereoptical views especially and I thought the broken country around the Lassen Peak should be photographed because it could not be shown satisfactorily in drawings. In later years King was the first to carry out these ideas on a large scale; and now the camera is an indispensable part of the apparatus of field work in surveys. Many similar instances might be given in which King did the things of which others had dreamed."[38]

In 1865–66 King and Gardner were with General McDowell in Arizona and sharing high adventure on that frontier. One day on a reconnaissance they were trapped by Apaches near Prescott, and the braves forced them to undress to be spread-eagled. Gardner was for fighting his way out but King persuaded him to wait. It would have been suicide to try and fight more than fifty bloodthirsty warriors, all of whom had rifles and revolvers. After whispering to Gardner, King calmly went up to one of the braves and began working a cistern-barometer, explaining in Spanish this was a new-type range rifle the cavalry was using. The warriors started to gather about when the cavalry appeared and they fled.[39]

There is no evidence of how King met O'Sullivan after the war but possibly one of the generals or officers he had met in Washington recommended the lanky Irishman. O'Sullivan now was well known to the men and officers of the

Army of the Potomac through Gardner's *Sketch Book of the Civil War* and a large collection of stereo prints of the war, most of which were credited to O'Sullivan. King must have heard that O'Sullivan was a brilliant and courageous photographer.

Recalling Professor Brewer's advice that photography was necessary for geographical surveys, King hired O'Sullivan and told him to report to New York in the spring.

King, meanwhile, gathered his corps of scientists. Not only must his men be the leaders in their fields, but they had to be dedicated to his project, in perfect health to stand the rigors of the mountains and plains for three years, and sufficiently well adjusted to get on together. Young Gardner, his close companion and friend of the trail, was his first appointment. Gardner turned down the chair of geodesy at the Lawrence School at Harvard—under the supervision of the famed Whitney—to accept King's offer. In geology, King selected the Hague brothers, James Duncan and Arnold. Samuel Franklin Emmons, a friend of Henry Adams and a graduate of the Royal School of Mines and the École des Mines in France, was next. Thus the geological branch of the Fortieth Parallel Survey now had four young men, all educated in New England and private schools and at Harvard and Yale. James Hague was the oldest at thirty-one. Several young scientists were hired along with a man to study the fauna along the Parallel. This was Robert Ridgway, who had never been to college. He was the son of an Illinois village pharmacist.

Ridgway, only sixteen at the time, was hired at the suggestion of Spencer Baird of the Smithsonian Institution, who had been corresponding with the boy for years on ornithology. In March 1867 Baird wrote to the boy offering him a job at the Smithsonian. He also asked him: "How would you like to go to the Rocky Mountains and California for a year or two as a collector of specimens . . . there would probably be a salary of about $50 a month and all expenses necessary . . ."

Ridgway responded immediately. His choice was the West.

Ridgway was with the King Expedition for more than two years in the field, collecting 1522 specimens of birds. In later years he would become the curator of birds in the United States National Museum and the author of more than five hundred scholarly papers. King had made another shrewd choice of a dedicated follower.[40]

In the next three years young Ridgway and O'Sullivan would team together on many side expeditions.

King was anxious to leave but there were countless details to be cleared up before the party left New York. Scientific instruments had to be purchased, packed, and shipped, a military escort must be provided for, and money—hard money, for only gold was recognized on the frontier—gotten out of Washington.

The scientific gear was purchased and General A. A. Humphreys, Chief of the Army Engineers and ostensibly King's superior, placed five to six thousand dollars in gold at his disposal. Major General H. W. Halleck, commanding the Military Division of the Pacific was ordered to furnish King with twenty mounted men and provisions and the Quartermaster General's office was instructed to give the party what supplies it needed.

That spring O'Sullivan was also busy selecting a complete photographic outfit, glass plates and chemicals, and packing them for shipment. Then King had a brief illness which delayed the group for a week in New York. On May 1 Gardner, the Hague brothers, and some others went on ahead and eleven days later King, O'Sullivan, young Ridgway, and the others sailed on the huge Pacific Mail side-wheeler *Henry Chauncy* for Aspinwall, Panama.

There was no fanfare. The New York *Times* of May 2 gave them fifteen lines on page eight and that was all the attention this gallant little band of young scientists received for embarking on a project that would take them years to complete, at enormous personal hardship and sacrifice.

At Aspinwall they crossed the Isthmus—which O'Sullivan would know firsthand a few years later—and boarded another side-wheeler, the *Constitution,* for Panama City.

Years later some of them told a humorous story of how King was given an infant to hold by its mother, who promptly disappeared. The story says King cared for the child during the long train ride, then turned it over to a colored woman in Panama City. This woman would figure in a strange story years later.[41] The child, it seems, supposedly ended in the employ of King as a servant. If anything, the story is apocryphal.

In June the entire party was reunited in San Francisco. From there they pushed on to Sacramento, where they found a "pleasant camp ground." For the next three weeks King purchased supplies, mules, horses, and wagons. O'Sullivan selected an old Civil War type army ambulance as his traveling darkroom and two mules—"a cantankerous black" to haul it and an experienced packer. They loaded the mules and the ambulance with over two hundred pounds of chemicals, plates, and cameras and were ready to go.

On July 3, 1867, O'Sullivan swung his ambulance into line as King led his United States Geological Expedition of the Fortieth Parallel into the Western wilderness.

The young scientists in King's party were in robust health, starry-eyed and city-soft. With the exception of King and Gardner, who knew the mountains, few of them had been west of the Mississippi, some not even past the borders of their own states. But all were highly educated and cultured, many spoke several languages, and the classics had been part of their lives since boyhood. This is the company in which Tim O'Sullivan, son of Irish immigrants, country boy and Civil War photographer, found himself. But if he didn't have their polish he had something that all of them must have admired, even envied. O'Sullivan knew life, death, suffering, courage, and cowardice firsthand. How many men did they know who could boast of having been at Gettysburg on the second morning when the mists had rolled over the wheat and the glorious dead, or who had ducked the bullets of the Rebel sharpshooters at Fredericksburg, or who knew how it felt to cringe behind the gabions at Fort Hell when the guns of Malone were sending over shells every few minutes?

As Gardner later said:

"Fifteen men from all grades of society; from all parts of the Union; of every age and disposition are not exactly made a homogeneous party at first . . ."

But O'Sullivan, the Civil War campaigner, said it better:

"To know a man you must campaign with him."[42]

The survey's geological and geographical aims concerning the Fortieth Parallel centered in the area where Nevada's western border begins its southwestern slant. The Parallel lies forty or fifty miles south of the Great Salt Lake while the transcontinental railroad was to pass north of it. In 1869, when his party had moved westward to where Cheyenne is located today, King had to veer north from the Parallel in order to touch the railroad.

It was and still is a vast and forbidding country. Several years before Mark Twain had crossed its desert area, "the hubs of the coach wheels sunk from six inches to a foot. Men and animals were coated with dust until they were all one colorless color."

"There is not a sound—not a sigh, not a whisper, not a buzz, not a whir of wings, or the distant pipe of a bird! not even the sob from the lost souls that doubtless people that dead air . . ."[43]

King's final report includes a description of that lonely land where O'Sullivan was to spend the next three years. According to Soreno Watson, one of the scientists, the area explored was bounded on the west by the high Sierras and the Washee Mountains which crossed the border into Nevada. Eastward, the original survey was carried into the Wasatch Mountains where O'Sullivan took some memorable pictures. The regions between the Sierras and the Wasatch Mountains had two main depressions: one at the base of the Sierras; the other, Great Salt Lake Basin. The Truckee River—on which O'Sullivan would almost lose his life—flowed into the saline Pyramid and Winnemucca Lakes. The Carson River formed a lake on the border

The King camp near Salt Lake City. By O'Sullivan.

of the Carson Desert where an extensive "sink" or alkaline mud flat, twenty to thirty miles in diameter, was also located.

In the Great Basin the longest and most important river was the Humboldt, which provided the route for three hundred miles of the Central Pacific through the mountain ranges. The Great Basin was a weird, lonely place of eye-numbing white flats, rats, scorpions, tarantulas, saline wells and springs, and rattlesnakes —once O'Sullivan waged a personal war against them—and a few tribes of miserable, diseased Paiute Indians. White men were few, most of them Forty-Niners who scratched a living out of the land by raising hay, cutting timber, or finding a few nuggets.

The survey party slowly made its way into this land. In mid-July Sergeant W. A. Martin, with "nineteen well mounted and armed men," joined the party as its army escort.[44]

The survey teams quickly fell into an ordered routine. A camp was established, tents erected, and the American and Fortieth Parallel flags raised with a brief ceremony. Then the various parties of scientists were sent out. These camps were used on an average of two or three months to give the scientists a chance to collect their specimens while the geologists and topographers used the base camp as headquarters and received reports from their side parties.

King's executive ability and shrewd judgment of the men he had selected kept the camp on an even keel. Everyone, from cook to trooper, had a task to perform. There were disputes and petty arguments but King and Gardner usually managed to soothe the ruffled feathers.

That first season the party worked from dawn to dusk, examining rocks and fossils, and climbing and measuring crags and peaks. Side parties, usually with O'Sullivan as a member, ranged far and wide across the wastelands of western Nevada. Slowly the geological and topographical map of the Fortieth Parallel began to take shape. In O'Sullivan's mounting collection of photographs, the vast, harsh beauty of this fantastic wonderland began to be recorded.

At one point King was troubled with desertions from his cavalry unit. One trooper, a notoriously bad character who had given King a great deal of trouble, finally deserted. King was determined to make an example of this man and set out after him with Sergeant Martin. The trooper had twelve hours head start but by riding all that day and night they crossed the range and came upon him preparing breakfast. King took the man prisoner at pistol point and brought him back to camp. From there an escort took the trooper to Sacramento and Alcatraz.

Another time King tracked a huge grizzly for several miles and finally found him in a deep cave. His fellow hunters warned him not to go into the forty-foot-deep cave but King insisted they needed fresh meat. He crawled into the hole until he saw the bear's glowing eyes and then fired. A trooper got so excited he hauled out King by the feet, bouncing him over the pebbles and rocks until King's face looked

Virginia City mine, by O'Sullivan.

as if it had been clawed by a bearcat. But the bear was skinned and the survey party had bear steak that night.

Somewhere a huge Negro, described as "soft spoken and polite," "adopted" King and became his servant. In later years he traveled all over Europe with King. One day, as the story goes, King was standing on the edge of a crag overlooking Grand Canyon.

"What do you think, Joe?" he asked the Negro.

"No place for a gentleman, sir," was the reply.

In the late summer the party stopped off at Virginia City, that high-riding boom town where the mounds of whiskey bottles were as high as a cabin's roof. There were a few muddy streets, clapboard houses, and plenty of hard-drinking, hard-rock miners with money in their pockets from working the Comstock Lode. Here in this sprawling bonanza town O'Sullivan made photographic history. He carried his equipment down "several hundred feet below sunlight" to photograph the inside of the mine, using a pile of magnesium as a flashgun.

O'Sullivan wasn't the first to take a picture

Waldeck, the Cincinnati photographer, who took the first known underground photographs in Mammoth Cave, Kentucky, his two friends who accompanied him, and their equipment. Note the giant reflector on the left.

underground—Charles Waldeck of Cincinnati did this the year before in the Mammoth Cave—but O'Sullivan was the first to take the interior of a mine. The photographs are remarkably clear, the flare of the bright magnesium catching the miner, pick in hand, working on a vein. Above his head is a stub of candle stuck in a beam.

It is obvious O'Sullivan took these pictures at great personal risk. Surely he knew that the flare of the unpredictable magnesium hundreds of feet deep in the bowels of the Comstock Lode could touch off a pocket of inflammable gas, killing them all and collapsing one of the richest silver mines in the world . . .

After a stopover at the mine, O'Sullivan, young Ridgway, and several other members of the survey, traveled to the Truckee River, a cold, swift stream that empties into the southern portion of Pyramid Lake. O'Sullivan managed to

O'Sullivan undoubtedly got the idea of using burning magnesium wire to make sufficient light for underground pictures from the photographs taken by Charles Waldeck, whose well-known photographs were described by the editor of one photographic journal as a "miracle" of photography. This is a rare interior shot of the cave, the first of its kind.

get a small bateau, named the *Nettie,* and they set off for the lake, about twenty-five miles distant.

The *Nettie,* probably built by a local resident who had come from New England, was, as O'Sullivan called her, "a perfect model of her class . . . a single glance was all that was necessary to convince a man reared on the rugged coast of New England that the craft was the handiwork of an artisan who had built boats for New London fishermen."[45]

The mules were left behind and O'Sullivan's plates and chemicals stored aboard with Ridgway's instruments. According to O'Sullivan this was the first time the Truckee had been navigated "with such a craft," so for a time the trip was delightful and adventurous.

The *Nettie* took the early rapids with ease and sailed with the grace of a swan across the long stretches of still water. But as they approached the lake the sounds of the rapids grew louder, ominous, and more menacing. There had

The Nettie, *on the Truckee River. By O'Sullivan.*

been a great deal of laughter and joking but this soon died away. All eyes were on the hissing water that slid over the smooth rocks like sheets of green glass flecked with cream. As in a sudden frenzy, it leaped against half-submerged rocks and sent curtains of spray high in the air to sparkle in the strong sunlight. Once the trunk of a tree shot past the boat and they watched as it was whirled about like a cork and sucked down in a huge whirlpool.

Suddenly the *Nettie* was gripped by a strong current and slammed against two rocks, which held the boat fast about forty yards offshore. The oars were ordered out, but the current swept them away. Then the sweeps were tried, but the tough ash "bent into shape more like an ox-bow yoke."

It was finally decided that someone had to swim ashore to fasten a line so the *Nettie* could be pulled free. O'Sullivan, a powerful swimmer, volunteered. He stripped to his underwear and dived into the roaring water. While the men in the boat held their breath, O'Sullivan fought the rapids. At times he was hidden by the spray, which blew over his bobbing head. Then a shout went up. He was seen crawling ashore a hundred yards down the rapids. Most of his underwear had been torn away and he was battered and bruised. Slowly he made his way upstream until he was abreast of the *Nettie*. Several unsuccessful attempts were made to throw him a line. Obviously a weight was needed.

One of the excited helpers picked up O'Sullivan's pants, containing his pay—three hundred dollars in twenty-dollar gold pieces—and this was used as a weight. The rope reached O'Sullivan but the wallet had vanished.

"That was rough," he recalled, "for I never found that 'dust' again although I prospected a long time, barefooted, for it."[46]

The line was made fast to a spur of rock and the *Nettie* was swung free. Half-foundering, it was hauled ashore.

The wet and thankful party bailed the boat out and made camps among the rocks and underbrush. The next day they set out for the lake, this time passing the *Nettie* hand to hand along the edges of the wild rapids.

Pyramid Lake was like a place that time had forgotten, a blank spot in some prehistoric calendar. The surface of the lake was rough and stormy, then suddenly clear and sparkling. The sheet of water, some thirty miles long and twelve miles wide, was studded with huge, rocklike pyramids, some five hundred feet high, their sides covered with a strange calcareous tufa which O'Sullivan said resembled a "vegetable growth of vast size."[47]

O'Sullivan found the pyramids varied with the light. At some moments the huge mounds seemed to possess a rich, warm tint, other times a cool gray hue. They scaled the largest pyramid only to find themselves in a colony of hissing rattlesnakes:

"From every crevice there seemed to come a hiss. The rattling too was sharp and long continued. The whole rock evidently was alive with rattlesnakes."

They fought the snakes but there were too many. Finally they abandoned the rock "to the serpentine tribe."[48]

Apparently O'Sullivan and the others fished for a time because he reported they caught a couier, "a sprightly fish having the color of salmon and quite as game . . ."

They also caught trout, "not precisely the speckled beauties of the Lake Superior region; neither do they bear a close resemblance to the sluggish, black spotted trout of our southern states. But it is a trout, nevertheless, which rises to the fly and is a pleasing morsel . . ."

While O'Sullivan took a series of pictures of the weird and striking lake, Ridgway made his studies and the party started back to the main camp. No one wanted to pull the *Nettie* back up the rapids so horses were hired at an Indian reservation and the party started back across some of the most forbidden land in the nation.

Hints of trouble first appeared when young Ridgway complained to O'Sullivan his mule was so huge it felt as if he were riding a high-peaked roof. Then the mules stampeded and Ridgway was almost thrown. The next morning the boy mounted another one and the party started out for Humboldt Sink. Ridgway still continued to have mule trouble. Now his animal refused to stay with the others. It jogged ahead, with Ridgway kicking and sawing at the reins.

Heat waves made the country shimmer, as the party moved on in high-noon silence. Suddenly O'Sullivan saw Ridgway slide from his mule, tie it to a brush, then curl up in the animal's shadow. When O'Sullivan and the others reached Ridgway, they found he was burning with fever—malaria—the vicious "mountain ail" that would hit them all.[49]

As Ridgway later wrote:

"I never knew when they picked me up and placed me in the ambulance, nor was I conscious at all until camp was reached."[50]

The party was now approaching the Humboldt Sink, one of the most horrible places in the deep West. Its approaches are of volcanic rock, stacked like piles of lava matchsticks, making it almost impossible to get through with a mule train and ambulance.

As O'Sullivan recalled:

"The rocks present an unbroken outline which may be pleasing enough to the eye, but to journey over with pack mules is laborious and difficult to the extreme. The foothold is very insecure and danger from fragments of rocks that are frequently dislodged by those who are in the advance is continually experienced by the climbers in the rear."[51]

Ridgway never forgot that terrible place. Many years later the stench, the putrid water, the hordes of mosquitoes were still etched in his memory:

"The marshes were miles in extent and almost entirely covered by a dense growth of tule (a large bulrush of the American Southwest) except where the river meandered through now and then expanding into a small lake. These marshes were surrounded by a bare plain, con-

O'Sullivan's wagon and mules in the wastelands near Steamboat Springs, Nevada. His camera is at left.

sisting in the winter season of mud, but at this time baked perfectly dry and hard by the heat of the sun, except in the more depressed areas, which were covered by a deposit of snow-white alkali. From these extensive flats, desert plains lead away to the barren mountains on either side, whose summits are bare and rugged eruptive rocks of weird forms and strange colors. Upon the whole, the entire region was one of the most desolate and forbidding that could be imagined, and in these respects is not surpassed by any other portion of the land of alkali or the everlasting sagebrush. The effluvium from the putrid water and decaying vegetation of the marshes was at times sickening, while at night the torments of millions of the most voracious mosquitoes added to the horrors of the place."

O'Sullivan undoubtedly was now in charge of this side party. This arrangement was to become almost routine on all the side expeditions.

The days and nights in the Sink were almost unbearable. The swarms of mosquitoes were so great they extinguished the candles, the water so sulphurous it stunk like rotten eggs, while the heavy, stagnant air was so heavy with the rotting tule, it gagged the man who took a deep breath.[52]

While the party inched its way across the mountain crest, O'Sullivan paused many times to take pictures which give a vivid idea of that weird world of volcanic rock and lava deposits.

"It was a pretty location to work in," he recalled, "and viewing there was as pleasant work as could be desired; the only drawback was the unlimited number of the most voracious and poisonous mosquitoes that we met on our trip. Add to this the entire possibility to save one's precious body from the frequent attacks of the 'mountain ail' (malaria) and you will see why we did not work more up that country. We were in fact, driven out by mosquitoes and fever . . ."

By early September nearly all the camp, including O'Sullivan, was stricken. Conditions were so bad King moved his camp from Wright's Canyon to Unionville, Nevada, "in order to place sick men, who at this time numbered about three-fourths of our whole party, under shelter, for the barometer indicated the approach of a great storm." King later told General Humphreys that, once, out of fifty men he had only three available men.[53]

While the members of his party fought off the malaria attacks, King, O'Sullivan, the topographer Clark, one soldier, and "Son," chief of the Humboldt Paiutes, headed for a mountain range west of the Reese River, almost in the heart of central Nevada. Here King was almost killed by a lightning bolt, which numbed his right side. He was carried back to camp where he stayed for a week.

From central Nevada the main party continued the survey across the desolate land while Ridgway and O'Sullivan returned to the Sink. At last, by what King called a "tremendous effort," the first season's work was finished and the party moved back to Virginia City just before Christmas, the mules and O'Sullivan's ambulance-darkroom crunching through two feet of snow.

King estimated he and his men had covered a stretch of country "the most difficult and dangerous I know of on the continent"—including the boundary of California (120° West), as far east as the second Humboldt Range (about 117°30′ West), and from the southern boundary at 39°30′ North to the northern boundary at 41° North.

"The party," King reported, "are all well and united by a healthy esprit de corps."

O'Sullivan spent the winter of 1867–68 at Virginia City, where he took more pictures of the Comstock Lode and the mining camp. While he took winter photographs and catalogued and packed his plates, the scientists classified their collections and wrote up their field notes.

Spring finally arrived and the snowbound mining camp was at last set free. Now with the bitter winds blunted by the soft breath of spring, O'Sullivan set up his tripod to take the rugged mountains, snows still creaming the peaks, in the crystal-clear morning air.

In Virginia City and Carson City twelve miles away, the Fortieth Parallel party began to organize its gear. O'Sullivan had new supplies of glass plates and chemicals, his mules were winter-fed and frisky, the iron-rimmed wheels of his ambulance greased. On the tenth, King announced his plans for the coming year. The expedition this season would be divided into three sections. The areas this time would be central and eastern Nevada and western Utah. The great Western names ring like bells in his report of that year: New Pass, Shoshone Mountains, Reese River, Toyabe Range, Fort Ruby, White River mining district, Overland Road, Salt Lake City Desert, Din Don Pass, Clear Valley, and Antelope Pass.

King was eager to get started. Once he was in the field there was no hesitation.

"We are in the saddle generally by 6 A.M. and work until sunset," he reported to Washington.[54]

There were Indian alarms this year. Once an outlaw band began raiding along the Truckee River and the alert spread by friendly Indians saved some of the party, including young Ridgway, from a massacre. Another time in northwestern Nevada, Ridgway's group was surrounded by a band of hooting, yelling Shoshones and the party cocked their rifles, but "Capt'n Frank," the Shoshone chief, produced a letter which indicated he was friendly.

The chief and his band stayed that night. There were presents, a pipe was smoked, and

O'Sullivan lined up the savage-looking band for photographs.

When King's party reached the Ruby, Toyabe, East Humboldt, and Clover Mountains they found the passes still clogged with snow.

Now there were new hardships for O'Sullivan and the others to face. Last year there had been the Humboldt Sink with its terrible hordes of malarial mosquitoes and stinking water. This year there was the thin, rarefied air of the mountain passes that seared lungs like cold fire, and the treacherous snow that swallowed men and mules in seconds.

Some of the drifts were thirty to forty feet deep. It wasn't unusual to see a heavily laden mule sink abruptly out of sight.

King decided the only answer to the problem was to travel at night so the frozen snow crust would hold the weight of his men and their mules.[55] But sometimes, in the brilliant moonlight, at, say, three in the morning, a mule would suddenly vanish and O'Sullivan and the others would spend hours roping the kicking animals to haul them up from the deep holes in the snowdrifts.

"In one instance," O'Sullivan recalled, "not less than thirteen hours were consumed in crossing a divide, and the whole distance traveled did not exceed two and a half miles."

The thin air gave the party trouble. "It is not difficult," O'Sullivan wrote, "to learn that the mule which made an easy burden of a pack at the altitude of 2000 feet above the Pacific could not bear the same burden over any long trail at the height of 10,000 or 11,000 feet."[56]

The party continued to cross the mountains, camping until midnight or later when they reached a snow line, then moving cautiously across the frozen crust. Only then could the mules and men "make it possible to take a trail which would otherwise be quite impractical."

The memory of those bitter nights when men and animals gasped in the thin, frigid air as they inched upward, always remained with O'Sullivan.

"The party endured indescribable hardships," he recalled in his strongest statement regarding his experiences in the Western mountains.[57]

But if he recalled the hardships, O'Sullivan also recalled the striking beauty of the mountains, particularly the snow lakes in the upper reaches, large basins of clear, cold water that shimmered and sparkled in the brilliant sunshine, more than nine thousand feet "above the surf that rolls upon the shores of the grand Pacific coast."

O'Sullivan also stopped off at Fort Ruby, a desolate frontier post. Richard Burton, translator of the *Arabian Nights* gives an excellent insight into the rugged existence O'Sullivan must have led during the time he stayed at Fort Ruby.[58] Burton had stopped at Ruby and the Overland stage station just east of the fort on his tour of the West in the 1860s. He wrote:

"While the Shoshone is tracking and driving the old mare, we glance around at 'Robber's Roost,' which will answer for a study of the Western man's home. It is about as civilized as a Galway shanty, or the normal dwelling place in central Equatorial Africa. A cabin fronting east and west, long walls thirty feet, with port holes for windows, short ditto fifteen; material, sandstone and bag limestone slabs compacted with mud, the whole roofed with split cedar trunks, reposing on horizontals which rested on perpendiculars. Behind the house a corral of rails planted in the ground, the inclosed space a mass of earth, and a mere shed in one corner the only shelter. Outside the door the hingeless and lockless backboard of a wagon, bearing the wound of bullets—and resting on lentels and staples, which also had formed parts of locomotives, a slab acting as stepping stones over a mass of soppy black soil strewed with orkes of meat, offals, and other delicacies. On the right hand a load of wood; on the left a tank formed by damming a dirty pool which had flowed through a corral behind the 'Roost' . . .

"Beneath the framework of the bunks were heaps of rubbish, saddles, cloths, harness and straps, sacks of wheat, oats, meal and potatoes, defended from the ground by underlying logs; and dogs nestled where they found room. The floor, which also frequently represented the bedstead, was rough, uneven earth neither tamped

O'Sullivan's ambulance-darkroom in the Ruby Valley. By O'Sullivan.

nor swept, and the fine end of a spring oozing through the western wall kept it in a state of eternal mud . . .

"The chairs were either posts mounted on four legs spread out for a base, or three legged stools with seniform seats. The tables were rough dressed planks . . . The walls were pegged to support spurs and pistols, whips, knives and leggins . . . Soap was supplied by a handful of gravel and evaporation was expected to act as a towel . . . Rifles, guns and pistols, lay and hung all about the house, carelessly stowed as usual, and tools were not wanting—hammers, large borers, axe, saw and chisel. An almost invariable figure in these huts is an Indian standing cross-legged at the door or squatting uncomfortably close to the fire . . .

"These savages act as hunters bringing home rabbits and birds, we tried out revolvers against one of them and beat him easily; yet they were said to put, three times out of four, an arrow through a keyhole forty paces off."

Burton was writing of the crude Overland stage station, but the fort itself was far from luxurious. There were split-pine bunks and fleas. Wind moaned through the chinked log walls, and the food was crude and rough. Days never seemed to end. The monotony was maddening. However, there was an occasional "ball" to break the long months, and O'Sullivan, a handsome man, undoubtedly waltzed and reeled some of the ladies at the post. He took a series of plates of Ruby and not even a century can dispel the stark loneliness of the crude log huts, the barren, windswept parade, and the morose privates of the Indian fighting army of the 1870s.

In the Ruby Mountain chain, where they spent almost two months, O'Sullivan took many photographs of the peaks and of Ruby Valley, where a marsh was the home of thousands of birds. The tule was so thick that streams feeding the marsh could only be seen from the heights. More than once O'Sullivan pointed his camera down the lonely valley and took the streams that twisted in and out of the dark green marshes like winding silver bands, while above him great gardens of Indian paintbrush, gilias, blue pentstemons, and delphiniums stretched to the snow lines.[59] One wonders what O'Sullivan could have done with modern color equipment.

For months O'Sullivan and his mules wandered in and out the valleys and canyons of the Ruby chain. Occasionally he would meet a few Paiutes gathering the pine-nuts which grew in the vicinity. The wedge-shaped nut was tossed in a fire to char the tough outside shell. The nut was then dried and pounded into a coarse meal. Cakes were baked in ashes, "much like the manner the hoe cake is by the Negroes of the South," O'Sullivan recalled.[60]

One day King heard about the deserts, more than a hundred miles south of the Carson Sink, and asked O'Sullivan to photograph this desolate region. This time the ambulance, drawn by four mules, was used instead of his pack mules. The traveling darkroom was not only more comfortable but it enabled O'Sullivan to carry large amounts of water to make a number of views.

O'Sullivan's first impression of the sand mounds was being adrift in a vast, silent world of enormous mounds of snow. In the searing sunlight the white sand sparkled like a frozen winter's crust.

"The contour of the mounds," he recalled, "was undulating and graceful, it being continually broken into the sharp edges by the falling away of some of the portions of the mound, which had been undermined by the keen winds that spring up during the last hours of daylight and continue through the night."

O'Sullivan and the party spent a few days in this strange world of moaning winds and shifting sands. He trudged from mound to mound, the sand rolling away from under his boots to be caught up by tiny whirlwinds that twisted and danced across the sparkling, hard-white surface.

O'Sullivan took several pictures of the mounds. Once, in order to capture something of the immensity and loneliness of the place, he climbed to one of the highest mounds and photographed his ambulance and mules below, dwarfed by the towering giants.[61]

O'Sullivan rejoined the main party, which was moving eastward along the Overland Stage Coach Road. Later they left the road and moved northward toward the Snake and the great Shoshone Falls.

Here O'Sullivan took some of his most striking photographs. The falls, smaller than Niagara, have a series of breathtaking cascades roaring through vast rock walls, worn and twisted into many weird shapes. The following year O'Sullivan described how he took his striking views:

"The surroundings of the main falls are such that any number of views can be taken of the scene.

"Standing upon the craggy rocks that jut out and form the walls of the tableland below the falls, one may obtain a bird's eye view of one of the most sublime of the Rocky Mountain scenes. Even in this section which is many feet above the falls, the air is heavy with moisture, which is attributable to the mist into which the river's great leap shivers the water.

"From the position on the crags you also have a grand view of the different falls, of which the main one seems but the culmination. Each small fall is in itself a perfect gem in a setting of grandeur in the glorious masses of rock. On one great wall can be traced a tolerably perfect outline of a vast figure of a man. The whole form is not less than one hundred feet in height.

"There is in the entire region of the falls such wildness of beauty that a feeling pervades the mind almost unconsciously that you are, if not the first white man who has ever tred the trail, certainly one of the very few who has ventured this far.

"From the island above the falls you may not see the great leap that the water takes, but you will certainly feel sensible of that fact that you are in the presence of one of Nature's greatest spectacles as you listen to the roar of the falling

A dramatic view of O'Sullivan's wagon and mules in the California desert. By O'Sullivan.

water and gaze down the stream over the fall at the wild scene beyond . . ."[62]

Studying O'Sullivan's superb photographs of the falls, one can easily imagine him perched on the towering crag, the chill air sharp and distinct as clear ice, solemn, looking out over the roaring water, the sullen sentinel rocks, the billowing sea of green, the glinting ribbons of distant streams, and saying to himself, "I am the first . . . the very first . . ."

O'Sullivan and the party worked until mid-October of 1868, when they reached the Great Salt Lake. The men of the survey had carried their topographical and geological work over a belt one hundred miles wide and five hundred miles long from the Sierras to the shores of the Great Salt Lake. Among other things, they had demolished the myth of the so-called "desert coal-field" and a survey had demonstrated that the Goose Creek coal region in northwestern Nevada was only a legend.

"Summing up this year's work," King reported, "I may conscientiously say that it has been an entire success."[63]

The camps were broken up before the first frost and the equipment stored in Camp Douglass near Salt Lake City. Now for the first time in eighteen months O'Sullivan and the survey men left the mountains and the barren plains for the comfortable East. Each man was given a thirty-day furlough before reporting back to King in Washington. Their new headquarters were now in a brick building at 294 H Street, where that winter the results of the survey would be classified and written up along with next year's plans.

We don't know how O'Sullivan spent his furlough but undoubtedly he saw Gardner and Brady in Washington after a visit with his father on Staten Island.

Washington now was changed from the Civil War boom town O'Sullivan had known. There was a new regime, Grant was President, the streets were paved, the hogs and chickens had

A close-up of Shoshone Falls. By O'Sullivan.

disappeared, and new mansions dotted the side streets. Even the Congressmen, as E. L. Godkin reported, "were wearing clean shirts almost every day."

There were street cars on Pennsylvania Avenue, the uniforms were gone, peddlers seemed to be everywhere selling potatoes and oysters. Willard's was still the busiest place in the city with rows of hacks tied up at the hitching post, ready for customers.[64]

If O'Sullivan saw Brady, and there was no reason why he wouldn't, he must have been struck by the aging of the master of photography. Brady's eyesight was worse, his business had fallen off considerably, and he was deeply in debt to the Anthonys for chemicals and plates they had given him for his Civil War work. Brady had thousands of plates but no one was interested in the war anymore. At the time, Brady was contemplating giving the Anthonys a large part of his collection in payment for some of his debts.

Very little seems to have gone right for Brady after the war ended. Three years before, he had staged an exhibition of his prints at the New York Historical Society and though the prints had been praised the exhibition was a financial failure. As a last measure he had been forced to sell the last few parcels of property in New York's Central Park section.[65]

Brady's catalogue of war views had been published. It listed some seven hundred scenes of battle areas and more than twenty-five hundred portraits. Most of the scenes were made in Virginia within traveling distance from Washington. Of the remaining, about fifty were made

Salt Lake City with Camp Douglass on the left. By O'Sullivan.

in Tennessee, Georgia, South Carolina, and at West Point, New York. O'Sullivan undoubtedly saw some of his photographs—still credited to Brady.

Gardner had also issued his *Photographic Sketch Book of the Civil War,* with forty-two of the one hundred beautifully mounted albumen prints credited to O'Sullivan.

The profits of the Brady gallery now had slipped badly. When O'Sullivan and the Gardner brothers were operating it the gallery had yielded $12,000 a year, plus the $4000 from Anthony and Company from the sale of the war negatives. Before the war ended, Brady's books showed only a profit of $4860 and $276 from Anthony.[66]

But Brady still had confidence that the Civil War plates would some day be valuable. He kept storing all he could find, even making copy prints of the prints in Gardner's *Sketch Book* and George M. Barnard's *Photographic Views of Sherman's Campaign.*

But the public refused to buy Brady's war albums, even though he reduced them from $75 to $50.

O'Sullivan undoubtedly heard of the trouble Brady had had with Jim Gibson, Brady's former wartime photographer, who had met O'Sullivan many times. Before the war ended Brady had sold one half of the gallery to Gibson for $10,000, accepting $5000 in cash and four promissory notes. In July 1864 a number of suits were filed against the old photographer in the District of Columbia for nonpayment of wages, failure to pay his rent, and for carpenter work on the gallery.

In order to gain control of the gallery Brady consented to proceedings in bankruptcy and the gallery was sold at auction in July 1868, with Brady buying the gallery back for $7500 with court approval.

Gibson insisted that Brady had allowed the gallery to run into debt "for the publication and manufacturing of certain photographs to be used for campaign purposes." It was the making of a composite photograph of the impeachment managers for the trials of Andrew Johnson and another of the Supreme Court Justices which had run them into heavy debt. Gibson claimed he had sent many letters to Brady in New York informing him of the financial crisis but Brady had never answered. Gibson then took out a mortgage on Brady's gallery without notifying Brady. The court action was still pending when Gibson left Washington to settle on the Kansas frontier and Brady returned to his gallery, which he now was forced to operate on a reduced scale.

In the year O'Sullivan returned to Washington from the West, Brady selected another manager for the Washington gallery. This time it was A. Burgess, a photographer and well-known gunsmith. Burgess began building up the business and once again the celebrated and famous posed in Brady's Washington gallery—among them Grant and Mark Twain.

O'Sullivan found Alexander Gardner back from the Kansas frontier and they certainly must have swapped tales of the West—Gardner telling of the wild cow towns with the first herds coming in and the railheads edging across the plains, and O'Sullivan of the deeper West and the Humboldt Sink, the deserts and the mighty Shoshone Falls.

There is little doubt that those who knew O'Sullivan noticed how he had changed. He was still slender, but he had a mustache and the wind and suns of the high mountain country had dyed his face to the color of old leather.[67]

O'Sullivan reported to King that winter. The reports were being prepared for General Humphreys and Congress. There would be volumes of O'Sullivan's prints, so his task that winter was probably the selection of plates and captions.

By mid-May the survey party was back in Salt Lake City with King. Gear had been repaired or replaced, and the stock purchased. This season King again split his party into three teams. His group was to work the north end of the Great Salt Lake, another group the south, while a third was to survey the lake itself.

O'Sullivan and Ridgway accompanied the survey of the lake, which took more than two months. It was the first survey made since the one in 1849–50 by Captain Howard Stansbury of the Topographical Engineers. It was not without danger. Twice King and his little boat, the *Eureka,* capsized and the men nearly drowned. The water they swallowed almost choked them and they had to cling to the capsized boat until rescued.

Large masses of decomposing grasshoppers covered with alkali dust were mistaken for land and O'Sullivan and the others found themselves knee-deep in decaying insects, the stench so horrible they were almost asphyxiated. Then hordes of flies, "about half the size of a house fly," plagued them until the survey men thought it was almost as bad as the Humboldt Sink.[68]

By late summer the survey had been in Echo Canyon in the Uinta Mountains in the Valley of the Provo and at the headwaters of the Weber River. Later King described this part of the survey as a sort of triangle, with the Uintas running east and west, forming the south side, the Wasatch Mountains running north and south, forming the west side, and the Green River roughly delineating the third side. Within the triangle was a desert more barren than any they had ever encountered.

O'Sullivan apparently left the Salt Lake survey teams to join the surveyors and geologists who moved into the Uinta Mountains, an immense block of mountains running about one hundred and fifty miles long with ranges as high as 11,000 feet. Unlike any other range in North America it quickly rose to a horizontal plateau summit, forty to fifty miles wide, covered with ponderosa pine, Engelmann's spruce, Douglas-fir, juniper, and aspen. The view, from O'Sullivan's photographs, shows ice-worn canyons, open green pastures, and glacial lakes.

The season finally ended in September and King announced that the three-year survey had been finished. The stock and gear was sold at auctions in Virginia City and Salt Lake City and the workers were paid off. King stayed until late autumn but Ridgway and the other scientists left for the east in September. O'Sullivan probably joined them. Now he would temporarily abandon the West for the jungle.

DESERT COUNTRY

The desolate flats of the Great Salt Lake Desert.

The Falls of the Provo in Utah.

The big bend of the Truckee River with the expedition in camp. This was just after O'Sullivan swam through the river's rapids to save their boat.

Lake Marion in the East Humboldt Mountains.

Cottonwood Lake in the Wasatch Mountains.

The City of Rocks in northern Utah.

A view of Snake River.

A member of the expedition bathing in one of the hot springs. This may be Clarence King.

mid Lake with its strange rock mounds.

The astronomical observatory, probably near Fort Ruby in Nevada.

Long Ravine Bridge on the Central Pacific Railroad.

SHOSHONE FALLS

The brink of the falls, with a member of the expedition peering out over the rushing water. The glass-like appearance of the water is probably due to the long exposure.

An overall view of the falls.

The main falls and upper or "Lace" Falls.

A close-up view of the main falls, with a member of the expedition standing at the edge of the cliff.

MINERS AND MINING

One of the series of historic photographs taken by O'Sullivan several hundred feet below the surface in the Comstock Mine, Virginia City, 1868. O'Sullivan took photography's first pictures in a mine by igniting magnesium wire to obtain sufficient light. It was a risky business in a mine undoubtedly filled with gas pockets. When O'Sullivan took his photographs the Great Comstock was at its zenith.

A miner in the Comstock Mine, caught by O'Sullivan's camera in the glare of the burning magnesium.

Cave-in at Comstock Mine.

A miner at work in the Comstock Mine.

Gold Hill Mining Camp, Nevada.

Sugar Loaf Mining Camp, near Virginia City.

IMPERIAL
EMPIRE
18

The Montezuma Silver Works, Oreana, Nevada.

The mining town of Austin, Nevada.

The Summit Mine, Belmont, Nevada. This is typical of the many small mines dotting the countryside of the Comstock Lode.

Ore wagons coming down the trail at the Savage Works, Virginia City.

Quartz mine in Meadow Valley, Peroche, Nevada. Note the horse used to raise the derrick.

Brick ovens at the Montezuma Silver Works, Oreana, Nevada.

The Kearsage Mining Works, an engraving based on an O'Sullivan photograph and typical of the kind used to illustrate some of King's and, later, Wheeler's reports.

The summit of the Wasatch Mountain Range. The King Expedition had great difficulty crossing the snow line of the range, O'Sullivan recalled in 1868, because men and mules sometimes disappeared in forty-foot drifts. King was finally forced to travel at night in the moonlight when the crust of the snow had hardened.

O'Sullivan's camp in the Upper Cottonwood Canyon in the Wasatch Mountains.

5

CAMERA IN THE JUNGLE: THE DARIÉN SURVEY EXPEDITION, 1870

"You have opened to the world an almost unknown wilderness, you have procured information that others before you have sought for and failed . . ."

Lieutenant Commander Thomas O. Selfridge, Commander Darién Survey Expedition, in General Orders to the members of the survey party, April 13, 1870

There was no rest for Tim O'Sullivan. He still refused the quiet, mannered galleries of Washington and New York where the great and near-great came to have their pictures taken by Brady or Gardner. This was a time of beginnings and he wanted to be part of it.

Clarence King was back in his Washington headquarters on H Street putting together the huge reports for General Humphreys. There wasn't anything for O'Sullivan to do—no more Western plains or high mountains or vast stretches of salt flats that glittered like roadways of diamonds.

But there was another expedition being formed, this time to explore the Isthmus of Darién (Panama) for a possible canal route. King probably heard about it and recommended O'Sullivan to Lieutenant Commander Thomas O. Selfridge, chief of the expedition. On January 11, 1870, O'Sullivan was hired as the expedition's official photographer at five dollars a day while in the States and seven dollars a day on the expedition.

The expedition had formed in the summer of 1869. In the last days of that year Selfridge was at Annapolis preparing a list of supplies for Secretary of the Navy George Robeson. Among the items were a thousand pounds of preserved beef, and corn, chicken, butter, rubber blankets, leggings, fish hooks, matches, and flints. The list, Selfridge told Robeson, would be enough for one hundred and twenty-five men for eight months.

As Selfridge's official correspondence shows, he miscalculated on supplies. At one point he was forced to order a guard to prevent the men from filching stores of the advance parties in the jungle.

Evidently he had taken a lesson from the Army on the Western frontier, where gifts were necessary in dealing with the Indians. On January 7 we find Selfridge asking Robeson for a large number "of gifts for the Indians." These included beads, spool cotton, and drill cloth of many colors.[69]

Selfridge pointed out to Washington that no

Navy Department
Washington Jany. 11. 1870.

Sir:

You are hereby appointed Photographer to the Darien Surveying Expedition.

You will proceed to New York and report to Lieut. Commander Thos. O. Selfridge, commanding U.S.S. Nipsic and the Expedition, for duty.

While in the United States your pay will be at the rate of five dollars ($5.) per day, and during the absence of the expedition,—from the date of sailing,—your pay will be at the rate of seven dollars ($7) per day.

You will mess with the ward room officers and quarters, bedding and mess expenses will be be found you by the government.

Traveling expenses will be allowed you when traveling under orders. All these expenses will be paid out of the appropriation for the survey of the Isthmus of Darien.

You will consult the Coast Survey for a proper outfit of apparatus and material for your work, and have everything ready to be placed on board the vessel by January 16th.

You will conform to all the rules of Naval discipline.

Very Respectfully
Geo. M. Robeson
Secretary of the Navy.

Timothy H. O'Sullivan, Esq.
Photographer
Washington D.C.

O'Sullivan's letter of appointment as photographer to the Darién Surveying Expedition, signed by Secretary of the Navy George M. Robeson.

vouchers were acceptable in the jungle so Robeson assigned him $8000 "in coin."

In mid-January O'Sullivan traveled to New York and purchased cameras, stereos, and the larger models, chemicals, and glass plates from Brady's old suppliers, the Anthonys. The final bill was $300.34. The crated materials were delivered to the Brooklyn Navy Yard and placed aboard the U.S.S. *Guard,* assigned as the expedition's storeship. O'Sullivan had his quarters and darkroom aboard the *Guard.*[70]

Lieutenant Commander E. P. Lull, commanding officer of the *Guard,* was ordered by Selfridge to leave Brooklyn by January 15 and sail for Aspinwall (now Colón), Panama. Lull was advised to seek out the "headman of the Indians and advise him the chief of the expedition would be on hand shortly."

O'Sullivan came aboard on the twelfth along with several other civilian members of the survey, the crew, and a small detachment of Marines. On the morning of January 15, 1870, the *Guard* cast her lines and set out to sea for Panama. It was a rough journey with a rough crew. The *Guard*'s log recorded several violent incidents. Twice Lull was forced to put men in irons in the brig and on bread and water. One entry has a crewman striking an officer.[71]

While the *Guard* was nearing Panama, Selfridge was finding himself harassed by bureaucratic red tape. Someone had failed to assign a Navy vessel to be stationed on the Pacific side of Panama and Selfridge sent off a tart note to Robeson pointing out the ship was vital in shuttling supplies to the survey teams in the jungles. A ship was finally assigned, the *Nyack.*

Selfridge and his staff set sail for Aspinwall in February aboard the U.S.S. *Nipsic* accompanied by the U.S.S. *Nyack,* Lieutenant Commander Thomas Eastman commanding.

Bad luck hit the expedition almost from the start. Before it arrived at Aspinwall the *Nipsic*'s engines failed. Selfridge ordered a stopover at Porto Bello, where it took weeks to repair the damage. Before the *Nipsic* left, Selfridge tried to hire bearers or laborers but found they refused to enter the jungles "for fear of the tribes."

"I fear I may have trouble with them (the tribes)," he wrote to Secretary Robeson.

This surprising statement ends the letter:

The Nipsic, *Lieutenant Commander Selfridge's command ship. By O'Sullivan.*

"But if they compel me to hostilities by an armed opposition I shall not cease till every cocoanut tree between Caledonia Bay and San Blas is destroyed."[72]

It was the old, sad story of the military philosophy toward the Indians whether in the Isthmus of Darién or on the plains—the only good Indian is a dead Indian.

When he arrived at Aspinwall in late February, Selfridge ordered Eastman, commander of the *Nyack,* to sail around the Cape to the Pacific to make a survey of the Gulf of San Miguel and ascend the Sabana River as far as the Lara and make surveys of both rivers.

"Let me impress upon you the necessity of kind relations with the Indians," Selfridge wrote Eastman. "Upon their good will will depend much of the success of this expedition."[73]

In mid-February the first surveying party left the *Guard* under Lieutenant G. C. Schulze. It consisted of two other officers, a surveyor, a mineralogist, surveymen, twenty-five marines, and ten coast natives who finally had been persuaded to enter the interior.

Selfridge warned Lieutenant Schulze against molesting Indians or entering their villages.

"Go out of your way to gain their friendship," he wrote Schulze.

Hatchets were issued to every fifth man for "blazing the trail and no singing or noise must be permitted after dark."

On the morning of February 25 O'Sullivan joined the first large reconnaissance party led by Selfridge himself. There were sixty Marines, ten seamen, several officers and native bearers.

As Selfridge wrote Robeson:

"While I did not consider this large force necessary for mere protection, I judge its display would produce a beneficial effect upon the Indians, would accustom the men to the country, would disabuse them of the imaginary dangers that we have heard so much of, and would enable me to judge personally of the difficulties of the work and hold interviews with the mountain tribes, also to ascertain how far I could count upon their opposition to our plans . . ."

It was a terrible mission. They climbed the cordillera, moved down the Subcutí River and into the Indian villages. They advanced foot by foot, with "machete men cutting the trail."

The deep, rapid streams were crossed human chain fashion, in waist-deep water. After the rivers and streams came the cliffs, some more than a thousand sheer feet, which had to be scaled by ropes and clinging fingertips.

"After a time," Selfridge wrote Robeson, "the men had to throw away everything but their provisions."

#8. U. S. S. Nipsic,
Caledonia Bay, U. S. of C.,
February 22d, 1870.

Lieut. G. C. Schulze,
U. S. Ship "Guard",
Caledonia Bay, U. S. of C.:

Sir:

To you will be entrusted the command of the party for the survey of the route starting from Caledonia Bay.

In placing you in this important situation I must impress upon you, that to you more than to all others, will depend the success of the work to be done by your party.

Many and great obstacles you must expect to meet, but none that perseverance, patience and courage cannot overcome.

You will ever remember you are moving in an unknown country, the inhabitants of which may or may not be friendly, and you must proceed with caution and at the same time endeavour to gain their good will by kindness and forbearance.

You will not permit your party to straggle or to enter any village, but pass on one side of it. Any outrage upon their women will be most severely punished.

Your party will consist of two officers besides yourself, a surveyor, mineralogist, such men as are necessary for the survey, a guard of twenty five Marines with an officer, and ten natives.

The quantity of provisions and equipments will be regulated at some future time, for the present it is intended that the party shall return to the ship every night.

You will keep a private journal, to be filed away with the documents of the expedition, containing a record of daily proceedings, with such notes as may from time to time suggest themselves.

The order of march will be, viz., the native or cutting party, half your force as a guard to them, the surveying party, and the remaining portion of your force as a rear guard.

You will blaze the trees on your route, for which purpose every fifth man will be provided with a hatchet. You may also have axes if you find them useful.

A guard of one fourth of your force of Marines will be posted at night, in charge of a non-commissioned officer, from sunset to daylight. Cooks must be selected who will carry cooking utensils.

They must be called in time to have coffee ready for the party at daylight.

You will then take up your march for the day, make another stop at 11 o'clock for breakfast, after an hour's rest, proceed; and go into camp about 4 o'clock and cook dinner.

Before dark the fires must be put out and you must move away to the locality selected for the night.

No singing or noise must be permitted after dark.

Note in your journal, products of country, kind of woods, nature of soil, climate, character and probable number of people, height of mountains, depth and current of rivers, botanical and geological specimens, &c.

The surveyor accompanying your party will give general directions for the course to be followed, and the work will be carried on as he desires, and conformable to his plans.

Bench marks will be from time to time selected and clearly described in your note-books, that your track can be taken up at any time.

Very Respectfully
Your Obt Servt
Signed Thos. O. Selfridge
Commander,
Comdg Darien Survg Expdn.

Commander Selfridge's instructions to Lieutenant Schulze of the U.S.S. Guard *for a surveying expedition of Caledonia Bay.*

After scaling the cliffs they found a small Indian trail which wound through deep gorges. At one point they came face to face with the fierce Subcutí tribes but Selfridge apparently made a show of force and "they turned conciliatory."

Then the rains came in solid sheets so that in a day not a man in the party had a dry stitch. One can only imagine the hardships O'Sullivan was enduring; in addition to keeping up with the party with his heavy load he must have had a horrible time keeping his plates and chemicals dry.

In the jungle the vines were thick and strong as steel cables. A path had to be hacked every inch and foot of the way in a steaming heat that sapped a man's energy.

The local natives Selfridge had persuaded by presents to accompany him proved worthless and he sent them back, replacing them with "jackasses to pack supplies to our party in the interior."

There is one reminiscent touch of humor in Selfridge's report. The Marines, like Marines everywhere, had a ready nickname for a land-

Members of the expedition in the field. Note machetes and sextons. By O'Sullivan.

252 Dr. Darien Exploring

1870				Amt. Ord.		5753 63
Apl	11	Salaries of Civilians & Laborers				
		paid up to date incl. viz				2487 97
		part Gold part Curry	1304.50 Currency 1183.47 Gold			
	7	Miscellaneous Expenses				
		paid up to date viz				9 70
		paid in Gold				
	28	Geo. J. L. Schroeter				
		50 prs Heavy Shoes	@ $3.00	150 00		
		5 Axe Handles	" .60	3 00		
		Transportation of Mail, Shoes &c		25 00		178 00
		paid in Gold				
May	2	Cabin Mess U. S. S. Nipsic Aspinwall U.S. of C.				
		To Messing Mr Arosemena of Columbian		37 00		
		Commn, 37 days @	$1.00 per day pd in gold			37 00
	1	Ward Room Mess U. S. Ship "Guard" Mandinga Bay U.S. of C.				
		Mess Bill of Civilians Employees of the				
		Darien Ex. Expn from Mar 1/70 to Apl				
		30th incl, 2 mos @ $40 per mo ea				
		J. A. Sullivan	2 mos	80 00		
		H. G. Ogden	" "	80 00		
		H. L. Marinden	" "	80 00		
		L. Karcher	" "	80 00		
		W. H. Clarke	" "	80 00		
		Calvin MacDowell	" "	80 00		
		A. J. Gustin	" "	80 00		
		J. P. Carson	" "	80 00		
		E. D. Bowditch	" "	80 00		
		A. T. Mosman	" "	80 00		
		T. H. O'Sullivan	" "	80 00		880 00
		paid in Gold				
	23	T. H. O'Sullivan Mandinga Bay, U. S. of C.				
		200 Stereoscopic Cards	2 25			4 50
		paid in Gold				
	30	J. S. Rider Mandinga Bay U.S. of C.				
		1 pr Shoes				3 00
		paid in Gold	Over			5753 20

The official record of expenses of the Darién Expedition. Note sums paid to O'Sullivan for "Stereoscopic Cards."

mark. This time a particular nasty gorge became "Rainy Hollow." It would bear this official name in all reports.[74]

In early March, Selfridge paid a visit to an old chief named "Shoemaker" on the River Diablo who wielded considerable influence with the tribes. After many presents Selfridge persuaded Shoemaker to send messengers to "the mountain tribes to secure their friendships."

A few of the plates in O'Sullivan's collection indicate he was along with Selfridge. Shoemaker and his braves look as ugly as the Paiutes O'Sullivan encountered in the Humboldt Sink section the year before.

It was now evident to O'Sullivan that it was almost impossible for him to make the photographic record Selfridge wanted. The camera was almost useless in the jungle because of the dense underbrush, the heat, and the heavy rain. O'Sullivan reported this to headquarters and was ordered back to the coast.[75]

As the weeks passed intelligence began to seep into Selfridge's headquarters aboard the *Guard* that trouble was brewing in the interior. In early March he advised Secretary of the Navy Robeson: "Native warfare may break out at any time."

To Robeson he gave the probable cause as Indian suspicion that any canal "will ruin their present way of existence."

Then came a sentence that might have caused eyebrows to raise in Washington:

"And they are right."[76]

In Washington at the time when the Army and general staffs were battling with the Quaker and other friends of the Plains Indians over broken treaties and promises, this blunt admission from the commander of an important expedition dealing with Indians was highly unusual if not shocking.

In March Selfridge appealed to the governor

Return of Commander Selfridge and his reconnaissance party from an expedition into the interior of Darién. An engraving based on an O'Sullivan photograph.

An Indian house on the Sassardi River. An engraving based on an O'Sullivan photograph.

The dense jungle was a photographer's nightmare. By O'Sullivan.

of Panama for laborers but even he could not persuade the local natives to enter the jungle "for fear of the tribes."

Selfridge then returned to the interior and after several days with the advance survey teams reported he could not find a pass over the mountains.

"Every step of the mountains has to be cut," he wrote, "the whole face of the land is broken and there is no such thing as a level open country."

By now O'Sullivan was confining his activities to the open country and native villages along the coast, rivers, and bays. On several occasions he snapped the entire expedition and the side parties as they came in from the interior.

He also traveled to the larger cities such as San Lorenzo and Cartagena where he photographed the inhabitants, interiors, and exteriors. As the months passed, O'Sullivan counted more than two hundred stereos and over a hundred glass plates.

Life aboard the *Guard* must have been boring and restrictive to O'Sullivan, accustomed to the free roaming life of the King Expedition. King was a far different commander than Selfridge; the scientist was a cultured, cultivated man even in the roughest sections of the West but he was never a stern task master. Selfridge was a scientist, but first a Navy officer.

Assistant Paymaster Loomis was ordered to make sure "not a single item be released from the stores without a receipt and such receipt be held against the officer until he returns them or accounts for their loss to me."[77]

Guards must be posted day and night, smoking must be restricted aboard ship, and accounts kept accurate.

Then turning his attention to the *Guard* and O'Sullivan and the other civilians, he ordered Loomis to make sure their mess bill was confined to "forty dollars and no more."

In April there was another Indian scare. Selfridge sent an advance party to "watch the Chuennas" who were reported on the warpath. Apparently the scare fizzled out. In a report to the Secretary of the Navy, he quoted one Indian scout as saying, "The Chuennas drink whiskey, they fight. No have whiskey no want to fight."

But as serious as the rumors of an Indian war were the stark realities of low provisions. The situation was so serious in April that Selfridge sent a runner to one of the advance parties in the jungle, ordering them to make sure that all supplies are guarded "and none must be taken or stolen."

Then in late April came an incident that almost finished the expedition. Selfridge was accused by a prominent Panama citizen of calling him a spy. In a letter to the President of the United States of Colombia, which included Panama, Selfridge hotly denied the charge of the "troublemaker" and informed him that when the maps of the survey were finished they would be placed at the disposal of his government by Washington.[78]

Despite the restrictions of weather, the jungle, and Navy discipline, O'Sullivan seems to have been busy. Several of his original plates indicate he ventured into the native villages, once taking his own picture beside some huts.* It shows a slender, handsome man with a sun-darkened face leaning on a large camera set up on a tripod in the muddy street of a village. His work must have increased, for the *Guard*'s log has Selfridge giving O'Sullivan an assistant at thirty dollars a month.

Selfridge reported to Robeson early in April that he doubted a canal could be cut through the Isthmus in the Caledonia Bay area, although he had finally placed his levels across the mountains "five hundred and fifty-three feet above the level of the Atlantic."

The task was performed, he reported, with great hardships. One was "a constant rainfall that fell in sheets." In his report Selfridge pointed out that a big disappointment was in photography:

"Few opportunities have occurred for using the photographic apparatus. There is much grand and beautiful scenery in the mountains but the dense vegetation has prevented me from using the instruments . . ."

* See page x.

Darién Harbor. By O'Sullivan.

But Selfridge pressed on. In June he reported to Washington he had surveyed the San Blas area and cautiously predicted this was the most likely spot for a canal crossing. The survey, he said, had been "retarded" by the continued heavy rains, but despite the weather his men had linked up with "a line" set up by another party sent out in 1864, "but not carried across the mountains."

"Connecting with this line," Selfridge wrote, "not only enabled me to verify the survey of 1864 which I found correct within a half mile, but gives a complete line of spirit levels across the Isthmus from ocean to ocean."

Selfridge then gave an idea of the hardships the men of the Darién Expedition had encountered in the jungle:

"This survey conducted in the rainy season has been made under much hardships and endurance. The country is broken up into deep ravines, with steep rocky sides, which in the wet season are so slippery that several were injured from falls, at other times the lines had to be run breast-high through rivers.

"In some parts of the dividing ridge the ascent is so steep, as to reach a rise of sixty feet in fifty feet of the horizon distance, and the observers were obliged to cling to trees to support themselves . . .

"The provisions and materials being exhausted, most of the expedition shoeless, and the men and officers pretty well worn out, I felt upon reaching the point on the Pacific slope connecting with the other line, that I had accomplished all within my means this season . . ."[79]

In June the *Nipsic, Guard,* and *Nyack* (which had returned from the Pacific) headed for the Brooklyn Navy Yard, arriving in July. O'Sullivan was paid and promptly went home for a visit. Then came more adventures in the deep West.

THE ISTHMUS

The Nipsic *in Limón Bay, at high tide.*

The landing at Chipigana.

The village of Santa Maria del Real, Darién.

Taking readings and sightings at the Tidal Station in Darién Harbor.

Turbo Village.

Street scene in Turbo.

A native hut in Turbo.

The main gate of the city of Cartagena.

A family scene in Cartagena.

e cathedral of Cartagena.

Sullivan titled this, "Inquisition." The assumption that the building was a prison was no doubt based on the bars on the windows.

The village of Chipigana with the Nipsic *in the background.*

The old Spanish fortress at San Lorenzo.

An intrigued group of natives at Chipigana.

An Indian rubber hunter.

The Great Falls on the Limón River.

Limón Bay, a superb view.

6

THE WHEELER EXPEDITION: 1871–75

". . . the boat party entered the jaws of Grand Canyon, not knowing what was before them . . . up to this time the rapids, though often very swift, had not been accompanied by heavy falls, and the estimate for the time to reach the mouth of Diamond Creek . . . was based on our experience up to that time, which supposed due allowances for increasing difficulties . . . subsequent revelations show how inadequate was this plan . . ."

"Mr. O'Sullivan, in the face of all obstacles, made negatives at all possible points, some of which were saved . . ."

Lieutenant Wheeler's journal, on the ascent of the Colorado River in the Grand Canyon, September–October 1871

There always seemed to be a Western hill for Tim O'Sullivan to climb, to see what was over the rim. Civil War, King Expedition, the Darién Survey—now another survey of the Western lands.

This time the survey would be commanded by an Army officer, not a civilian. It was all part of the Army's plan to revert from the police duty of the Reconstruction Era back to one of its former peacetime duties—the survey of the Western frontier.

When O'Sullivan returned to Washington the Army was in its darkest hour. The war-sick country had decided its military branches were expendable. By 1867 one of the most powerful striking forces in the world had been reduced from a million men in 1865 to barely 25,000 regulars. Now the country had an Indian-fighting Army, ready to try to break the will and spirit of the plains Indians.

The Indian-fighting Army was composed of galvanized Yankees, wanted men, immigrants and Bowery rabbits, and adventurers from all parts of Europe. One of the legends was that a command had to be given in three languages. Adventure and escape from prison or a powerful personal problem were the only motives to compel a man to spend four years in a windswept plains fort for less than fourteen dollars a month.[80]

It was more difficult to persuade West Point graduates to accept the Army as a career. Lieutenant George Montague Wheeler was one of the few who did.

Wheeler was graduated from West Point in the class of 1866. In a class of thirty-nine the twenty-four-year-old officer ranked first in philosophy and mathematics, second in engineering, sixth in mineralogy and geology, seventh in Spanish, eighth in ordnance and gunnery, ninth in ethics, and twenty-first in cavalry tactics. He ranked sixth in general merit.

The future was gloomy for this class of young new officers. Appomattox was a year past, Lee's

Army of Virginia and Grant's Army of the Potomac were rapidly becoming legends. The country was war-weary. It had enough of casualty lists, prison camps, parades, and high-sounding patriotic speeches.

A lonely Western post, forays against painted savages, monotony, boredom with little chance of promotion seemed the only possibilities for a young man seeking to make a career of the Army—an Army whose appropriations had been cut to the bone by an economy-determined Congress.

Despite this gloomy future Wheeler chose the Army as his career. Shortly after his graduation he was assigned to the post of second engineer on the survey of Point Lobos and vicinity in the San Francisco Bay area. On March 7, 1867, he was promoted to first lieutenant and a year and a half later appointed engineer on the staff of the Commanding General of the Department of California.

In 1867 Wheeler was exploring and leading reconnaissance parties in southeastern Nevada and western Utah. In that one year he covered 24,000 square miles of Nevada and 400 square miles of Utah. His principal assignment was to find a more direct route for the transfer of troops from Idaho, northern Utah, eastern Oregon, and Washington southward to Arizona. Previously the Army had moved troops by way of Pacific ports, southward by sea to California, then overland.

When he submitted his report on the surveys in Nevada and Utah, Wheeler suggested a general survey of the West, mapping the areas with a military eye, to include roads, railheads, mining camps, farms, villages, towns. In brief, maps which would serve the military to present "a thorough knowledge of the conformation of the obstacles and resources of a country."

Wheeler's proposal for another survey of the West would not overlap those made by King, Hayden, and Powell. Their maps had been "controlled by the theoretical consideration of the geologists." Wheeler was proposing maps that would include "astronomical, geographic, and topographic observations, with map delineations of all natural objects, means of communications, artificial and economic features, the geologic and natural history branches being treated as incidental to the main purpose."

Wheeler's suggestions were submitted to King's old friend, Brigadier General A. A. Humphreys, Chief of the Army Corps of Engineers, who was aware now how the civilian surveys had taken over the Army's traditional peacetime tasks, and also had received a generous slice of Congress' few appropriations.

Wheeler was summoned to Washington and in 1871 Humphreys announced the young officer had been placed in charge of a fourth Western survey.

His assignment was to take charge of a party which would explore "those portions of the United States Territory lying south of the Central Pacific Railroad, embracing parts of Eastern Nevada and Arizona" for the purpose of obtaining "correct topographical knowledge of the regions traversed and to prepare accurate maps of the section." Although topography was a main requirement, Wheeler and his men were also to ascertain "as far as possible, everything relating to the physical features of the country," the numbers, habits, and disposition of the Indians who may live in this section . . . the facilities offered for making rails or common roads, to meet the wants of those who at some future period may occupy or traverse this portion of our territory." In addition, the teams were to note mineral resources, the influence of the climate, geological formations, character and kinds of vegetation, its probable value for agriculture and grazing purposes, relative proportions of woodland, water, "and other qualities which affect its value for the settler."

Wheeler was authorized to employ ten assistants as topographers, geologists, and naturalists, in addition to packers, guides, laborers, and a photographer. The civilian employees were not to exceed thirty. Fifty thousand dollars was alloted for the expedition.

One of Wheeler's first selections was Tim O'Sullivan and a young debonair Bostonian named Frederick W. Loring, heir of a well-known Boston family, who ostensibly was going along as a "barometric observer and recorder"

Fred Loring. By O'Sullivan.

but whose real assignment was to publicize the achievements of the expedition in the Eastern press.

In the spring of 1871 Wheeler journeyed to Fort Halleck near Elko Station (also known as Halleck's Station), Nevada, where his survey team was ordered to gather. Several striking glass plates of this desolate little fort taken by O'Sullivan indicate he was already there or had accompanied Wheeler.

According to Wheeler's report, the party set out the first week of May 1871. The long line of mules, horses, and wagons moved across the badlands in heat that sometimes reached 118 degrees. When they found water late at night in dry beds of streams they knew it would vanish after sunup.[81]

By now surveys were an old story to O'Sullivan and he took countless photographs of the wild and desolate country. When the Paiutes and Utes appeared to act as guides to seek out the tiny springs, especially in the Death Valley country, O'Sullivan persuaded them to pose in bits of bemedaled uniforms they had received "from a journey to Washington." But there were times when some of the Apaches or Navajos refused to pose, insisting through an interpreter that the Shadow Catcher would imprison their spirits on his sleek, wet plates.

O'Sullivan seems to have taken more photographs of Indians on this expedition than at any other time. Staring out of his plates are the Coyotero Apaches, slender, impassive, dangerous. In contrast are the squaws and the old people, particularly among the Navajos. Evidently he spent some time among the tribes, probably on his lonely "field parties," to catch the women weaving rugs, families in camp, even newlyweds.

One of O'Sullivan's companions on the side field trips was Loring, the young Bostonian. He would send back two articles for *Appleton's Journal of Literature,* which were at times strained in their attempts at humor.

Loring's articles describe a council of war Wheeler had with Cowitch, a Shoshone chief. He made no attempt to disguise the contempt he felt for the half-naked braves and the vermilion-streaked chief he called: "An artistic barbarian with an eye for color."[82]

Loring wrote the reason for the council was "the supposition that the subject of our expedition was the massacre of all Indians in the state of Nevada—a supposition which had its foundation in the frantic behavior of our bug collector who scoured the mountains around us in search of prey."

Loring also had something to say about "Indian talk." He wrote:

"Indian talk is something like baby-talk in its utter disjointedness. Remember the style of conversation of Mr. Alfred Jingle, reader of Pickwick, and adopt it when you meet a big chief. Say "heap" as often as possible. Use it promiscuously with nouns, adjectives and verbs. Tell him he shall have a heap of muck-a-muck, assure him that he is a heap good Indian, and inform him that you a heap go away through the country. Omit all prepositions and conjunctions. Never say perhaps, but use as an equivalent 'maybe so.' The sign of equality too finds favor with the poor Indian's untutored mind. 'All

Shoshone Indians. By O'Sullivan.

the same as' is a phrase which is absolutely necessary to the success of any dialogue with an Indian. And, as a conclusion, the universal 'Sabe?' a word adopted from the Mexican vocabulary, must be employed.

"So our pioneer addressed the Indian: 'Heap good white man—camp—see Indian—want be heap friend Indian—white man all same as Indian—come up to camp—sabe?' "[83]

Loring, for all his show of sophistication, was a naïve young man; the Shoshone chief did understand the broken English and in fact sent for his interpreters "to reconnoiter."

Loring went on to describe the council with the Shoshone chief, his squaws and the braves putting on a show until Wheeler and his assistants "distributed the Indian goods in quite an abundance."

The Bostonian then tried to interview Cowitch "in the hope of obtaining some ethnological information . . ."

In broken English, Cowitch gave Loring some "ethnological information" for some cigarettes. At one point Loring tried to mystify Cowitch with O'Sullivan's camera but the chief apparently was only impressed when someone told him Loring was "the man who made newspapers."

"I could see that Cowitch was impressed, and I mentally apostrophized the glorious power of the press which—but I will save that sentiment for the next press dinner which I attend . . ."

Cowitch, that "grotesquely painted young chief" then allowed Loring to interview him for the next few hours, impassively discussing "ethnological problems" until Loring ran out of cigarettes.

Loring's conclusions reflect the philosophy of the frontier.

"It seems to me that I ought to draw some conclusions from the scenes of this day, and yet I dislike exceedingly to generalize. The Indian is a human being, and therefore capable of education and civilization. It is his right, even if he does not claim it, and it is the duty of the government and the people to give it to him. But the development of the country is also a duty and that philanthropy which denounces our settlers, who are hastening our work, as persecutors of the Indian, is as idiotic as it is ignorant.

"There are those who, through a sickly sentimentality or a love of notoriety, prate about the wrongs of the noble savage, who is, generally speaking, a filthy and degraded brute. This country is too valuable to humanity to be given up to grasshopper-hunting. The conduct of our settlers is not perfect, but it does not deserve opprobrious reproach. There are Indians who are harmless, and who are unmolested, to be sure, but also neglected, which is wrong. There are others who are blood-thirsty, untamed, and pitiless, and these are objects of attack, which is right. And certain would-be orators, who utter much meaningless stuff about the condition of the Indian in the East, which few there attend to or care about, are raising a bitter feeling in the extreme West, and may produce disastrous results in the future."[84]

The survey not only had its Indian councils but also a number of near-disasters, one in Death Valley. Wheeler, like King, Selfridge, and the rest of the scientists who conducted the Government surveys, seldom deviated from the stern, pedestrian prose of their reports, but Wheeler, in writing of this incident, forgot his military reserve.

"The route lay for more than 39 miles in light, white, drifting sand, which was traversed between 5 A.M. and 6 P.M., the center of the desert being reached about meridian. Two of the command succumbed near nightfall but after they were revived the march continued in the moonlight, until finally between three and four in the morning a 'living stream' was found by the Indian guides . . ."[85]

In the vast, deadly valley one of Wheeler's scientists almost died of thirst after wandering about the trackless wasteland for two days. He finally stumbled back into camp, "all senses but that of sight being gone . . ."

There was also a death, a member of the survey dying of consumption. Wheeler briefly mentions but doesn't describe it and for some reason —possibly because O'Sullivan was on a side field trip—there are no photographs, but surely it must have been a moving scene when the members of the survey gathered about to lower the corpse into the lonely Death Valley grave . . .

There must have been the scientists in their dust-stained clothes, the rough packers and mule skinners, the cooks taken from their fires, the impassive Indians, listening as Wheeler said the last words. Then perhaps a volley from the military escort as the dead man in a blanket-shroud was lowered by ropes. In that empty valley only the keening wind remained after the camp was broken and they moved on. One wishes Loring had some of the sensitivity of King or Emmons to create the moving scene hidden behind Wheeler's terse military report . . .

It was near Death Valley that O'Sullivan became involved in a mysterious incident that has overtones of violence and murder. There are only fragmentary news stories, obviously written by an embittered frontier editor but obviously the stories stirred the frontier until the Army was forced to conduct an investigation and subsequently issue a public denial. Curiously Wheeler never mentions the incidents in his official survey report.

The incident involved the disappearance of two civilian guides, William Egan and William Hahn.[86]

Apparently Wheeler had sent out side field parties as King had done and Hahn was one of the guides. The party returned charging Hahn had deserted and one of the survey team angrily told the townspeople that "had he time he would have returned to hunt and shoot him."

The newspaper item insisted, however, that instead of deserting Wheeler and the party, Hahn had been disabled and left to die by Wheeler's men, "for it was his pride to escort a party and could have no motive in abandoning it."

The item also described how the guide's saddle, blankets, food, and personal letters had been found "near the head of Death Valley in a canyon which has no outlet as it is evident that poor Hahn perished, as did his animal."

Then the item described how O'Sullivan and another member of the survey were guided some time later by another guide hired by Wheeler,

Death Valley, the scene of many hardships for the expedition, and where O'Sullivan was abandoned by his guide. By O'Sullivan.

William Egan, "a universally esteemed man well known throughout Nevada and this county."

Egan had been hired by Wheeler to guide the party from Swansea through Death Valley. They had proceeded as far as Telescope Mountain when Wheeler ordered a three-day camp.

During the halt Wheeler led a field party into the Telescope Mountains. Late that day he sent back word he wanted O'Sullivan to take a "small party" and join him in a canyon "to take a series of views." Egan, who was in camp, was ordered to guide O'Sullivan. The rest of the "party" consisted of a mule packer who "backed out to return to camp" after a few hours of walking in the suffocating heat.

At this point the mystery begins. According to the news account, O'Sullivan returned to camp but without Egan.

When O'Sullivan was questioned as to Egan's whereabouts he was quoted as saying:

"They came back but Egan went on."[87]

Wheeler returned to camp the next day and the newspaper charged "no inquiries were ever made as to what happened to Egan."

Peter Monto, a local blacksmith attached to the survey told the newspaper that Egan's pack animals and mining equipment were "appraised by Wheeler and taken over as government property."

The newspaper's editor set out to find answers to some questions only to be sent replies from "Wheeler's secretary, Loring, that are of the vaguest and most unsatisfactory description —saying something about Egan's starting from one side party to another in a locality entirely different, implying an uncertainty whether he reached his destination or not . . ."

The account detailed the search parties scouring the Telescope Mountains for Egan and also hinted that perhaps Wheeler had found a "location"—a mine strike—and had done in Egan to keep it a secret.

The long account made much of Wheeler's insistence that members of his party had to grant him their power of attorney "to represent them in anything that might be found" and wondered "Did the government fit out a private prospecting party?"

The expedition's camp near Belmont, Nevada. By O'Sullivan.

The newspaper account included another disturbing note, Wheeler's relationship with the Indians.

The account continued:

"Near Belmont (a mining camp in Central Nevada), the packers lost a mule, probably allowing it to stray, as they were not very closely herded. A boy was found herding cattle, who was taken to camp, and by Wheeler's orders, tied by the thumbs to an elevated wagon tongue, to make him tell the wherabouts of the lost animal.

"It is needless to say that the boy's tormentors succeeded in eliciting nothing but protestations of ignorance."[88]

The news item ended on another serious charge against Wheeler.

At Ash Meadow, some sixty miles from Death Valley, Wheeler had traded with some Indians during a five-day layover. Wheeler reportedly tried to get one of the Indians to "take a note."

In exchange the Indian wanted a shirt, a pair of pants, and five dollars. After Wheeler refused the Indian left, to return to camp the next morning with four braves.

The news account stated:

"The impetuous young commandant ordered them all tied to the ground, the Indians protesting they would "find the horses," seeming to think that some had been lost and that was the matter. They untied themselves and one of them tried to run. A dozen shots were fired at him and three of them took effect and subsequently the Indian died. The rest of them started out with the note, Corporal Magill and a private going along.

"In an hour they (the soldiers) returned, saying that the Indians had escaped with 18 shots flying after them. It is probable that they had no desire to keep the Indians, being afraid of being run into a rancheree. In this dilemma Captain Wheeler concluded in going himself, so taking an orderly he sallied forth. In the trip he was surrounded and placed completely in the power of twelve Indians, and only escaped with his life through the efforts of Salt, an "Indian Charley" (probably a half-breed interpreter) from Salt Lake, to whom intensive rations and goods were afterwards issued."[89]

The frontier editors in the vicinity of Death Valley continued their editorial attack on Wheeler in almost every issue. One front-page story charged Wheeler and his party with being "composed of brutes, if not worse."

The attacks continued long after Wheeler had left the valley, in fact after the survey had been disbanded for the season.

In late October an editorial in one weekly stated:

"Two guides taken from the Owen River country have never since been heard from, and the Inyo Independence broadly hints that they were murdered by members of the party . . . evidently the Wheeler Exploring party has disgraced the United States service, and had a few more of them met the fate of Loring,* they would have got only their just deserts . . ."[90]

Evidently the military at nearby Fort Independence heard the rumors and started an investigation, because one item has Major H. C. Egbert, commandant of the fort, writing to the editor to cautiously advise him he would look into the charges.

A later clipping reported that the search party moving through the Telescope Mountains had found some papers belonging to Hahn. The account bitterly charged that Hahn had died in the mountains and "Wheeler cannot be held blameless since he soon abandoned the search for the missing guide . . ."

A possible explanation of this mysterious chapter of the Wheeler Expedition, involving O'Sullivan, is partially explained in the yellowing files of the tiny weekly newspapers in and around Fort Independence.

In one, the Ely *Record,* is a long account of a letter from Charles King, one of the pioneers of the district and described as "well known to the community" commenting on Wheeler's expedition and the characters of Wheeler, O'Sullivan, and other members of the party. King praised them as men of "excellent reputations, zeal and enterprise." Wheeler, he said, was not only all of this but in addition was an officer "kind to his subordinates and the fitting leader of an arduous expedition."

In the files of the *Weekly Independent* is the final report from Captain Harry C. Egbert, Captain, 12th U. S. Infantry and commanding officer of Camp Independence, California, dated November 23, 1871. Egbert hints the stories were circulated by Peter Monto, the blacksmith, who might have been a disgruntled employee.[91]

Major Egbert quotes King's letter to the Ely *Record* praising Wheeler's reputation, then adds:

"I have no hesitation in believing him (King) before I would believe Mr. Monto, and in his opinion I have no doubt the community will agree . . ."

Then Egbert examines each charge:

"You state that Mr. Monto, in referring to Egan's supposed loss, says that 'Wheeler made some locations there and hints of a possible collision between the two.' In plain English, that Lieutenant Wheeler betrayed Mr. Egan in the desert and deserted him—that is, practically murdered him. If there is any man in our community mean-spirited enough to belie such a malicious fabrication, I pity him.

"Lieutenant Lyle told me that he had sent Hahn and Koehler, another civilian employee, ahead of his party for some purpose, for which I have forgotten, that when a long distance out, Hahn separated from Koehler, that the latter, keeping on performed his mission, and returned to the party but he never saw Hahn again. He particularly stated that a search was made for Hahn's trail but without success as Koehler would not identify the spot where they had separated."

Egbert then said that he recalled the mission the two were sent on by Lyle was a search for water, indicating that the party at the time in Death Valley might have been in difficulties.

Egbert continued with Egan's disappearance, quoting a long letter from Wheeler, written from Cottonwood, Nevada, in which Wheeler explained that Egan had set out with O'Sullivan to find Wheeler's party in the mountains but in fact had deserted O'Sullivan at Rose Springs "on the western slope of the mountains, west of

* Loring was killed by Apaches when he was en route to Washington with O'Sullivan after the Colorado River expedition.

Death Valley. The party had consisted of O'Sullivan, Egan and a packer who backed out and returned."

Wheeler wrote:

"We went out as far as we dared to go for him and are afraid that he may have been lost, although in the worst extremity of all the party he had the best chance of getting through."

Wheeler then begged Egbert to send him any information he had on Egan or Hahn "because I am anxious for them."

Egbert went on to say that Wheeler was also concerned "about Egan's mule and property" and would send a letter to one of Egan's friends asking him what he should do with the animal and mining equipment.

Then Egbert put an end to all speculation as to what happened to Egan:

"According to intelligence from the sheriff of a nearby county, Egan is alive and well in the Clark District."

He added: "I have written to Lieutenant Wheeler asking him for a reason for Monto's attack on him."

He ended with a grave warning that the articles by the *Independent* and other small weeklies obviously hostile to Wheeler for some reason, would seriously injure all Western surveys. Egbert pointed out that if the articles were reprinted in the larger Pacific Coast newspapers, which usually reprinted such sensational pieces, "It will be enough to prevent the granting of an appropriation on the one hand, or the Engineer's office from asking it on the other."

There is little doubt that Wheeler's expedition might have been highhanded in their dealing not only with the Indians but also the ranchers near Death Valley. A hint of this is found in a tiny clipping, pointing out that Lieutenant Lyle, attached to Wheeler's party, "took possession of a hay field of a local resident."

When the owner demanded the soldiers drive out their stock, Lyle supposedly "informed him to go to H—— and used language still more insulting."

The article ended:

"When the government is compelled to pay a thousand dollars damages (the suit is now being pressed) Lieutenant Wheeler may begin to think that citizens have some rights which are entitled to respect."

Loring's articles in *Appleton's* also enraged the local editors and at least one full column was devoted to denouncing this "Bostonian flop whose job with Wheeler is only to draw the 'long bow.' "[92]

There is little doubt the stories of the murder of the two guides, Egan and Hahn were malicious lies started by Peter Monot, the disgruntled blacksmith, and spread about the countryside by the embittered editors of the Inyo *Independent* who apparently had some unknown grudge against Wheeler and the survey. Why? Possibly because of Lieutenant Lyle's highhanded methods of trespassing local pastures and hay fields which were a source of livelihood to the settlers and the editor was voicing the indignation of his readers.

The problem of evaluating Wheeler's alleged cruelty to the Indians is another matter. Professor Bartlett, in his book on the Western surveys, wonders if Wheeler "did fall back upon military discipline and unnecessary cruelty in order to prevent his expedition from ending as a failure?"

This author is inclined to believe that's exactly what Wheeler did. Again it's the frontier soldier-officer philosophy; a good Indian is a dead Indian. In the post-Civil War period the military mind viewed the tribes as only pagan aliens in a land that belonged to the white man's railroads, towns, and cities. An indication that Wheeler's philosophy was no different is reflected in his writings twenty years later when he denounced the "peace at any cost" policy of Washington toward the Western tribes:

He wrote:

"The bones of murdered citizens cannot rise to cry out and attest the atrocious murders of the far-spreading and far-wide extending borderlands of the Great West, and while the fate of the Indian is sealed, the interval during which their extermination as a race is consummated will doubtless be marked . . . with still more murders, ambuscades and massacres . . ."[93]

The start from Camp Mohave, Arizona, September 15, 1871. O'Sullivan captioned this photograph: "Boat Expedition under Lieutenant Wheeler, the first and only one to ascend the Colorado through Grand Canyon to the mouth of Diamond Creek. Distance travelled: 260 miles in 31 days, with the boats often having to be portaged around rapids and drawn over rocks." By O'Sullivan.

Wheeler's party soon left Death Valley and the charges of murder behind to prepare for its next mission—the most spectacular, dangerous, and puzzling of the 1871 survey. O'Sullivan would be one of the few members of the team who would make it, but photographically it would almost end in disaster.

After leaving Death Valley, Wheeler led his party to Camp Mohave near where the California border runs into the Colorado. There was a short stopover at the camp as he waited for the arrival of three flat-bottomed boats and a barge from San Francisco.

His mission, he explained to his survey team, was to row, tow, push, portage two hundred miles up the Colorado River to Diamond Creek in the Grand Canyon.[94]

It is unfortunate that O'Sullivan did not catch the expression on the faces of some of the scientists and guides when they heard Wheeler's proposal. First, the journey was extremely dangerous, but more important it had little scientific value. Major John Wesley Powell had been down the river in 1869 and in 1857 Lieutenant Joseph C. Ives had been up the Colorado from the mouth to Black Canyon (about twenty miles south of the site of Hoover Dam) in an iron steamer. Wheeler explained that the goal of the expedition was to determine the limits of practical navigation, to measure the width and velocity of the river.

While they gathered gear and supplies, O'Sullivan made a series of pictures of the camp, local Indians, guides, officers, and quarters and the mountains and deserts in the area.

On September 16, 1871, O'Sullivan packed his camera, plates, and chemicals aboard a flat-bottomed boat which he named the *Picture,* then set up his camera on the rickety log dock.

When the three boats and barge had moved away from the dock he photographed the expedition's departure from Camp Mohave, boats and barge lashed together and oars up while several Indians and white men waved goodbye. Then he joined the *Picture* and the expedition began moving up the treacherous river.[95]

There were about thirty-five men, including boatmen, soldiers, Indians, and scientists.

The little-known journals of G. K. Gilbert, geologist and fourth scientist to be hired by the original United States Geological Survey, give a hint of the terrible ascent of the river. Gilbert apparently liked and respected O'Sullivan and many times they shared the command of one of the boats or side expeditions.[96]

The first day they made fifteen miles. In camp that night Wheeler formally made a treaty with the Mohaves accompanying the expedition. They were now in Paiute country, a nation warring with the Mohaves.

There was a feast and some dancing and the Mohaves and Paiutes, ostensibly friendly, "talked, laughed and gambled with each other in our camp." But on the thirtieth, a Saturday, Elitau, a Mohave who was friendly to O'Sullivan and Gilbert warned them "he had overheard the Piutes (sic) planning the shooting of the Mo-

O'Sullivan's boat, the Picture, *at the Black Canyon on the Colorado. By O'Sullivan.*

haves from ambush up the river. So we had a wild panic . . . and concluded to make camp tonight, though it cost us two hours of fair wind to wait for them to overtake us . . ."

Another council was held and peace declared.

On Sunday morning they set out again. By afternoon Gilbert and his party waited until O'Sullivan made a series of striking photographs of the "Cathedral," a six-hundred-foot rock formation. While O'Sullivan took his photographs Gilbert examined the sand and gravel and basalt formations and made his notes and sketches.

To catch up with the main party they rowed and hauled the cumbersome boats up a series of "long, stiff rapids" until even the moonlight could not help them feel their way.

For a week they rowed, towed, and pushed their boats and barge while O'Sullivan photographed the deep canyons and shot wild geese "for stewing."[97]

Gilbert wryly notes the goose was shot "by Hicox (99%) and O'Sullivan (2%)" Hicox was Frank Hicox the famous meteorologist.

They also met some Paiutes and Gilbert noticed uneasily that one of the guides "obtained from them a melon and some information that he did not divulge."

At Beaver Rapids, Wheeler's party had their first real taste of ascending the Colorado's rapids. Now it was only "percolating water that rises in a series of springs along the bank . . . and a great mass of gravel that blocks the river and makes three rapids . . ." but it was heavy, laborious work and the boats were finally hauled upstream by nightfall with the troublesome barge unloaded after it had swung wildly and seri-

The camp at the crossing of the Colorado just below Grand Canyon. Here the boats were met by two divisions of the party operating in the country north of the river. Men and supplies were transferred across the river. By O'Sullivan.

ously injured a member of the party and a guide.

Now they were entering the cañons and as Gilbert wrote:

"The wall has a right to all adjectives (except numerical) that have been given it . . ."

When they reached the crossing of the Colorado on Thursday, October 5, each boat was given fifteen days' rations for its nine men. Wheeler, O'Sullivan, and Gilbert were placed in command of the boats.

At ten the next morning they swam the mules across while Gilbert and Hicox climbed the wall of the cañon, but it was so difficult, Hicox had to return. After several hours of virtually crawling up the face of the cañon wall Gilbert reached the rim at sunset. He spent the night alone on the windswept peak and wrote simply by a small fire:

"Having no blanket I built a small fire in a sheltered spot among the rocks and hugged it all night, getting little sleep."

Gilbert spent most of the next morning sketching and examining the foot of the Big Cañon. He returned late in the afternoon "with a big tired on . . . but whiskey, coffee and rest brought me around however . . ."

While Gilbert was exploring the cañon's rim, O'Sullivan and Wheeler had advanced up the river. Gilbert joined them the next day and with O'Sullivan discovered some springs on the north shore and "named them . . . a large one of the Crater style O'S and I called Tufa Spring and Tufa Spring would be a good name for the group. Another large one with a fantastic canopy of tufa* is Grotto Spring. A third is the Baptismal Font. A fourth (now dry) and hanging against a large one is the Holy Water font . . ."

The expedition continued to ascend the river. Wheeler and Gilbert in the advance and O'Sullivan in the *Picture* about a mile in the rear. Later the *Picture* took the lead with O'Sullivan "photographing at will."

At Camp 21 they had their first near disaster. The rapids were fierce and one of the scientists was badly injured while an Indian guide had his cheekbone smashed against the rocks. A brief halt was called while the injured men were treated. It was an anxious day with Gilbert wondering if they could keep to their timetable "on such brief rations."

From Gilbert's notes O'Sullivan was constantly on the move, lugging his heavy camera and equipment up and down the steep washes that hugged the roaring rapids. Once he climbed a two-hundred-foot basalt ridge to photograph the river and later that day when he had rejoined the main party he described the area so minutely, Gilbert accepted his version and included it in his notes.

Wednesday, October 11, was disastrous. The lead boat unexpectedly rounded a sharp turn in the cañon and was swept into a fierce stretch of rapids. The boat was tossed about like a chip in a sluice. The scientists at the helm and on the long poles fought the roaring waters, frantically trying to dodge the rocks. For a time they were successful but suddenly the boat slammed against a rock and was swamped. The men, white and red, miraculously crawled ashore but the entire contents of the boat vanished.

* A porous rock formed as a deposit from springs or streams.

O'Sullivan, Wheeler, and Gilbert risked their lives in the rapids in an attempt to save the supplies but all they salvaged were a few blankets.

Gilbert wrote: "Saddle bags and . . . nearly all the rations were lost along with Lt. Wheeler's basket of papers and notebooks . . . some of the men are demoralized a little by the rapids and tomorrow I have volunteered to steer a boat up . . ."

On the thirteenth at Camp 22 in the Big Cañon the day opened "under a cloud." Gilbert noted: "It has been decided that some of the party discouraged and fearful of the rapids will return." Now it is only the *Picture* under O'Sullivan and the *Trilobite* under Gilbert and Wheeler that resumed the journey. The rapids became faster and much more dangerous. At times the boats were tilted so high "one must climb as though upstairs."

On Saturday the rapids were so fierce and the cliffs so narrow, rowing was impossible. Boats and supplies were portaged and the exhausted men fell on the sand and slept like dead men.

As they moved deeper into the cañon the air was filled with bats, their cries like legions of lost children, even loud above the roar of the water. It was almost like night in the deep crevice and, as Wheeler noted in his journal, the "rays of the sun never reached the boats."

At times when the rapids were passed the only sounds were their own grunts and groans and the whimpering of the bats "in a stillness like death" that depressed them all.

On the fifteenth Gilbert noted the question of rations was becoming desperate and "it was doubtful that we can fulfill them (boats) for five days . . . the question of rations may yet turn us back . . ."

The rapids were constant with few stretches of slack water. One day they hauled the boats from dawn to dusk, covering only four miles. When they rode the rapids the boats were roped together with hawsers but several times the sharp rocks cut the lines. Once when the lines to Gilbert's boat snapped, his boat roared downstream. Only the hawser caught in a web of rocks saved them from death or serious injury.

A towering wall in the Grand Canyon. Note the members of the expedition at the base. Many times O'Sullivan climbed such slopes to photograph the terrain after a day of tugging and hauling the boats upstream against the current. By O'Sullivan.

Painted Lake Camp in the Colorado Canyon where Wheeler halted the boats to prepare for the next day's ascent of the rapids in Black Canyon. By O'Sullivan.

On the sixteenth they ate the last of the rice and bacon and Wheeler put them on four pounds of flour a boat for seven men.

Gilbert noted grimly:

"This will last us until we reach Diamond Creek or back to the crossing—if that is possible . . ."

O'Sullivan was still taking pictures whenever he was relieved on the ropes or not carrying the "freight" on the portages. Apparently from Gilbert's notes he was never still, either waist-deep in the water, bent double on the ropes, or laboriously inching up some steep wash to photograph a curious basalt deposit or take a view of the camp or the river.

At a point called Double Rapids the rocks snapped the hawsers like twine and Gilbert's boat again made a dizzy descent only to slam against the bank on the wrong side of the canyon. O'Sullivan, Gilbert, and some of the Indians swam the river and, after two hours of backbreaking labor, pulled the boat back up the rapids.

They were now at a point in the rapids that Gilbert described as so fierce "only large boulders remained in the bed of the river." It was too dangerous to even stand in the shallow water at the edge, the party had to move up along the rocks, pulling "hand over hand."

On the seventeenth after a full day on the ropes they found they had covered less than three quarters of a mile. On the eighteenth the *Picture* swung loose and O'Sullivan and his party had a wild ride down the rapids. Fortunately the boat reached a pool of slack water and they could row and pole to safety.

On the nineteenth, provisions were dangerously low. Wheeler, now guarding the rations with a rifle, decided to send two of the party overland for provisions while the boats were calked. When they resumed their journey O'Sullivan's boat, the *Picture,* evidently had an accident because Gilbert mentions the expedition halted for a few hours "for O'S to dry things."

Later they found a "float," evidently some sort of raft, with a message attached from the overland party saying that Diamond Creek, their goal, was only six miles upriver.

This news cheered them all and they pushed on to reach the Creek late that night.

While the expedition continued on its last lap, a series of blunders almost ended in disaster for all of them.

Wheeler had ordered Gilbert and his companion to hurry ahead and contact the supply party waiting for them at Diamond Creek. Supplies could be sent back on horseback. But when Gilbert reached the spot where the supply party had camped, he was shocked to find it deserted.

Gilbert scribbled a note for Wheeler that he and his companion would attempt to catch up with the supply party. He placed the paper under a rock, then both men set off in the blazing heat.

In his diary Gilbert notes they walked from 10 A.M. to 10 P.M., "finally falling down exhausted."

For some unknown reason some members of the supply party returned and found the two men. After reviving them the supply party hurried back to the river, where a meal was served. Although he was exhausted and rail-thin from the terrible ascent of the river, O'Sullivan was still the photographer. The first thing he did after finishing his meal was to take Gilbert's picture "as a member of the *Trilobite* crew . . ."

Only twenty of the original party of thirty-nine had reached Diamond Creek. The nineteen that could not stand the hardships of the trip had returned to the base camp downriver.

O'Sullivan remained to the end. He had not only helped haul the heavy boats up against the fierce current, but also portaged and at least twice swam the rapids to salvage provisions and catch a runaway boat, in addition to carrying his heavy camera and equipment up and down cañon walls and basalt hills.

He had one last assignment. All during the ascending of the Colorado, O'Sullivan had been trying to persuade the Indian guides to pose but they were afraid. The Shadow Catcher, as the Indians called all frontier photographers and artists, might steal their spirits on his glass plates. While the others rested waiting for Wheeler to decide how they would return to Camp Mohave, Gilbert and O'Sullivan set out to somehow make the Indians pose. Gilbert said there was a great deal of talking and smoking but finally some gifts made the Indians agree to pose for O'Sullivan.

That afternoon Wheeler decided that some of the party would return overland in mule-drawn wagons and the others would ride the rapids for the two hundred miles down the Colorado. It had taken them thirty-three days to make their way up the river but only five days to return downstream to Camp Mohave, certainly a vivid demonstration of the powerful current they had ascended with three heavy boats and a barge loaded with supplies.

O'Sullivan had carefully kept his plates and equipment intact. He had hundreds of stereos and larger plates in small wooden boxes, certainly a vivid record of the thirty-three days the members of the expedition had towed, pushed, and portaged their way up the Colorado gorges. It was late October and Wheeler decided to abandon the expedition until the following year. Now must come the fruits of those weary days; he ordered O'Sullivan to leave at once for Washington where he hoped the photographs would impress Congress and the world. Loring would return East and write a series for *Appleton's* pointing up the bravery and courage of this military expedition.

Wheeler just didn't have King's luck. En route to San Francisco most of O'Sullivan's plates were lost, how we do not know. Then Loring started by stage for San Bernardino, California.[98]

At Wickenburg, Arizona, Loring boarded a canvas-topped stagecoach with two other mem-

Mohave Indian guides caught napping. The white man is probably G. K. Gilbert, the noted geologist and O'Sullivan's friend. By O'Sullivan.

bers of the survey. Among their fellow passengers was a jeweler from Prescott and "Moll Shephard, a disreputable character." Aboard was $25,000 in gold.

The stage rolled across the wasteland in a cloud of dust. Swaying and holding on to their seats as the big wheels bounced along the rutted road was the dapper Prescott jeweler, the two dignified but weary scientists, the disreputable Moll, and young Loring. The Apaches suddenly appeared when the stage was one hour out of Wickenburg. The driver laid on the whip but he died under the first volley, his shotgun messenger pitched to the road. Before the passengers had a chance the stage was riddled. Loring died with a bullet through his head, along with the two young scientists. The driverless stage careened down the road with the shrieking Moll and finally overturned. The only survivor was Moll, from which may be drawn a moral.

Thus ended Wheeler's dream that O'Sullivan's magnificent pictures and Loring's prose would persuade Congress that the military surveys, not the civilian ones, should receive the lion's share of any appropriations.

At first it was believed that the Indians had been painted outlaws, but later O'Sullivan discovered the killers were actually Apaches. There is one last romantic twist to the story of the "Wickenburg Massacre" as the frontier newspaper called it. One of the young braves in the Wheeler party had taken a liking to O'Sullivan

Maiman, the young Mohave scout, who hunted over a year for the killers of his friend Fred Loring. By O'Sullivan.

and Loring. In fact, he was one of the few Indians on the expedition up the Colorado who consented to pose for O'Sullivan. After Loring's death the scout spent a year seeking out Loring's Apache killers. They were later imprisoned by General Crook when he took over the Department of Arizona.[99]

The following year O'Sullivan's place was taken by Dr. Bell, an adventurous English physician who was an expert photographer. It is evident from Bell's plates he took only a fraction of the views O'Sullivan had taken the year before.

Where O'Sullivan went that year or what he did we don't know, but he did return to Wheeler's Expedition in 1873 and again in 1875. Wheeler's team now was sizable, at times eighty-nine officers and other assistants and an escort of seventy-nine men. But Wheeler never maintained the harmony King and his men knew; conflict between the civilians and the military was always just below the surface. From Wheeler's correspondence he was constantly writing letters soothing the temperamental scientists, who chafed under the military discipline which Wheeler insisted had to be part of every expedition.[100]

In 1873 and 1875 O'Sullivan was in the deserts and mountains of Arizona, Nevada, Colorado, and New Mexico. He knew Fort Defiance, Fort Whipple, Fort Garland, and particularly Fort Wingate. He froze in the mountains, knew the nagging thirst of the deserts, and walked through the carpets of bluebells in the deep valleys of the San Luis. His camera captured it all. In the Canyon de Chelly, where the mules developed large open sores because of the lack of grass and the horribly diseased squaws had to be driven from camp, O'Sullivan took unforgettable photographs of the pueblo ruins that are today embraced in the Canyon de Chelly National Monument. Here he used the same technique of vivid contrast he had employed when he had placed his ambulance in the vast emptiness of Carson Desert on the King Expedition. This time he had two members of the survey team climb the cliffs with ropes and pose on the now-famous White House ruins. In O'Sullivan's photograph the two men are pygmys in contrast to the awesome wall that rises thousands of feet above the valley, each stratum boldly outlined by the brilliant sunlight.

O'Sullivan took many photographs of this beautiful valley and the Navajos, who herded their sheep nearby, before the expedition moved on toward Fort Wingate, which was about twelve miles southeast of Gallup.

In the fall of that year the Zuñi Mountains, Santa Fe with its narrow streets of one-storied houses and women making cigarettes in the doorways and the busy public square would be captured by his camera.

Wheeler's correspondence in the National Archives shows he now regarded O'Sullivan much more than a photographer.[101] Several times during the summer of 1873 Wheeler appointed O'Sullivan "executive in charge of the main party" or directly in charge of field parties moving out of Fort Wingate or Camp Apache, Arizona. On July 15, 1873, O'Sullivan led "the main party" to the Zuñi and White Mountains on a trip that lasted from July 15 to August 30. After returning to Wingate, Wheeler wrote O'Sullivan he was to take on supplies for another journey north to the Canyon de Chelly,

The Humboldt Mountains, Nevada. O'Sullivan described it as a region of perpetual snow and recalled the crossing of this chain as one of the most exhausting experiences he had in the West. By O'Sullivan.

the Colorado Canyon between the mouth of the San Juan and El Navo de los Pavres, and the pueblos. At the conclusion of this expedition Wheeler ordered O'Sullivan to proceed to Santa Fe "for the purpose of obtaining certain views about military headquarters . . ." and to continue on to the survey's headquarters in Washington.

On another occasion Wheeler addressed a note to O'Sullivan "In Charge of Field Party" urging him to use "utmost economy" buying field supplies. That same year Wheeler, writing from Camp Wingate, issued orders appointing O'Sullivan, whom he described as "Civilian Assistant," as his agent for the survey in purchasing necessary supplies, not only at Wingate but at "any posts on his route as may be necessary to carry out the objects of the party assigned to his charge . . ."

Prior to this order, Wheeler had written to Louis Nell, Chief of the Triangulation Party headquarters in Santa Fe, advising him O'Sul-

One of O'Sullivan's famous views of the Canyon de Chelly, with an expedition member sketching.

livan had been placed in charge of "Party Number 4" during the march from Santa Fe to Wingate, "in order that you may be enabled to give more personal attention to professional duties."

He wrote:

"Mr. O'Sullivan will direct the supplying of the party and its movements, governed in these duties by the fact that certain trigonometrical points are to be occupied to accomplish the duties entrusted to you . . ."

From Wheeler's letters and dispatches it appears that the summer and fall of 1873 was one of the busiest of O'Sullivan's many years in the West. He was not only leading field parties and acting as an aide to the commander of the expedition, but was also taking numerous photographs from the deserts of Arizona to the canyons of New Mexico.

With the conflict between the military and the scientists increasing every year, perhaps Wheeler used the likable O'Sullivan as a sort of liaison between the two groups.

Before the end of 1873 O'Sullivan was known in almost every Western post from New Mexico to Arizona, not only as the survey's photographer, but also as Wheeler's official representative. In Wheeler's papers we find notes and orders to "forage agents" advising them to honor requests from O'Sullivan for forage, mules, or wagons.

Wheeler was an experienced officer and scientist who would be commissioned as the War Department's delegate to the Third International Geographical Congress and Exhibition at Venice. Among his party were many responsible, educated men and experienced military officers, yet he selected the shy, genial O'Sullivan as his official representative and purchasing agent, an obvious reflection of the photographer's integrity and ability to lead men.

In 1874 O'Sullivan again was missing but he returned to the West in 1875, for the last time. By now his large photographs published by the government in huge, gold-toned, hand-tooled leather volumes (some so heavy it takes two men to lift them), all part of Wheeler's official report on the 100th Meridian Survey, were attracting a great deal of attention from the public, the War Department, and Congress.

But O'Sullivan was weary. At the end of the 1875 expedition he said goodbye to Wheeler and headed East.

BACK IN THE WEST

O'Sullivan's wagon in the Humboldt Mountains. Note the guard, and O'Sullivan's high camera near the man in the chair.

A welcome addition to the menu—Elk. O'Sullivan at times brought in game, but as his friend Gilbert pointed out he was a better shot with his camera than with his rifle.

Lake Marion in the Humboldt Mountains of Nevada.

O'Sullivan camp on the edge of one of the many alkali lakes the Wheeler Expedition encountered in 1871. Note the salt deposit on the shore and the hunter trying for meat for the table.

Steam rising from a fissure near Virginia City, Nevada.

Witche's Rock, Echo, Utah. The small wagon on the right slope may have been used by O'Sullivan to haul his equipment to the site.

O'Sullivan's "cantankerous black mules" near the edge of the mouth of a geyser in the Pahute Mountains, Nevada, 1871.

Mountain transportation: mule, pack, and packers.

Cooley's Ranch, ten miles east of Camp Apache, Arizona, when O'Sullivan visited it in 1873. It was a characteristic mountain "park" and Apache Indian farm where the Indians grew corn, wheat, and a few vegetables.

One of the group of Pagosa Hot Springs showing encrustation on the surface. This was much prized by the Indians and miners because of its supposed healing qualities.

When O'Sullivan roamed the plains with King the buffalo herds were still making the earth tremble with their numbers. But in a b few years the herds were pitifully reduced.

ASCENDING THE COLORADO

The Wheeler Expedition ascending the Colorado, an engraving in the official report, based on an O'Sullivan photograph.

Iceberg Canyon of the Colorado looking upstream.

From the rim of the canyon of the Colorado River near the mouth of the San Juan River, Arizona.

The Grotto Spring, Grand Canyon, Colorado River, which Ó'Sullivan and geologist Gilbert discovered and named in 1871. O'Sullivan noted: "The water flows from the rocks above, and the umbrella-shaped rock about it is tufa, that has been formed by deposition from the mineral elements of the water. The light spot seen through and beyond is the sand beach of the river. Looking through this grotto is seen in the distance the walls of the Grand Canyon, 3500 feet in height on either side."

Looking across the Colorado River to the mouth of Paria Creek.

Black Canyon of the Colorado with O'Sullivan's boat, the Picture, *drawn up on shore.*

A striking view of the Colorado River from the rim of the Grand Canyon near Devil's Anvil. O'Sullivan had to scramble up the canyon's walls to take this photograph.

A riverside view of the towering walls of Black Canyon.

A view down Black Canyon from Mirror Bar, with the walls repeated by reflection.

A view of the Grand Canyon walls near the mouth of the Diamond River taken in 1871. O'Sullivan noted the distance from the water line to the first shelf is 1500 feet and from the shelf to the top of the table 8500 feet. The distance from the point of view to the top of the walls is three miles.

ARMY POSTS

"Camping Quarters" at Fort Ruby, 1868. O'Sullivan's caption probably means that these were the cabins used by the members of the King Expedition during that winter period when the scientists wrote their reports and O'Sullivan catalogued his glass plates.

fficers' quarters, Fort Ruby, 1868. Apparently building was going : at the time of O'Sullivan's visit. Note the lumber. Richard ırton, translator of the Arabian Nights *stopped off here on his ur of the West in the 1860s. His description of the stage station just east of Fort Ruby was terse and vivid: "about as civilized as a Galway shanty or the normal dwelling place in Central Equatorial Africa."*

parade of Fort Halleck, also called Halleck's Station, near Elko, Nevada. It was here that Wheeler assembled his first expedition in spring of 1871.

A government observatory near Fort Halleck.

Another view of the parade of Fort Halleck.

A sutler's store somewhere on the frontier, probably in the vicinity of Death Valley, taken in 1871. The store's sign read, "The First and Last Chance."

Commanding officer's headquarters, Fort Mohave, Arizona. This fort was built at the suggestion of Edward Fitzgerald Beale, leader of the famous "Camel Expedition" to survey a military road f Fort Defiance to California.

A section of the officers' quarters, Camp Whipple, Arizona. On some of his side trips, O'Sullivan bought supplies for the expeditio

Parade of Fort Apache built in 1870. Note field pieces.

distant view of Fort Apache.

The entrance to Fort Defiance, where O'Sullivan stayed many times in the early 1870s. Here he purchased forage and mules for the Wheeler Expedition.

Officers, their wives and children—and the nursemaid in the doorway in the officers' quarters, probably Fort Defiance. Note the baby carriage.

Paiutes at Pyramid Lake.

) superstitious Indians at Bear River. One, probably a squaw, her back to O'Sullivan's camera, while the other wrapped a blanket about his face so the "Shadow-catcher" could not capture his spirit.

The Mohave Indians of the lower Colorado, western Arizona region. According to O'Sullivan they were "the finest specimens in all the West, many of the males attaining the height of 6 feet."

Ute braves of the Kah-poh-teh band, northern New Mexico, "in full dress."

Pah-ge, a Ute squaw, of the Kah-poh-teh band.

Apache braves, as they appear ready for the warpath.

Shee-zah-nan-tan, Jicarilla Apache brave, northern New Mexico, in characteristic costume.

Pedro, captain of the Coyotero Apaches in his "Washington uniform."

Jicarilla Apache brave and squaw, lately wedded, Abiquire Agency, New Mexico.

Two Apache scouts and a member of the King Expedition on Apache Lake in Arizona.

One of the Coyotero Apache scouts who accompanied the Wheeler Expedition. O'Sullivan persuaded him to pose for a twist of tobacco.

An Apache squaw nursing her child in a carrying cradle.

An Apache squaw and her papoose.

A Navajo war dance performed for Wheeler's men at Fort Defiance, New Mexico, 1873.

A Navajo family. The women are working on one of the famous Navajo blankets which O'Sullivan noted was made of "native wool and bleached white."

Navajo boys and squaw in old Fort Defiance, New Mexico. In 1873, when O'Sullivan took this photograph, the fort was not occupied by troops but was instead an agency for the Navajos.

A Navajo brave and his mother. O'Sullivan noted: "The Navajos were formerly a warlike tribe until subdued by the United States troops in 1859–60. Many of them now have fine flocks and herds of horses, sheep, and goats."

The Navajos in the Canyon de Chelly. As O'Sullivan noted for this picture: "The squaw is weaving blankets on the native loom . . . and [they] are of the best quality."

A Navajo woman and child at their home in the Canyon de Chelly.

The old mission church at the Zuñi Pueblo, New Mexico. The view was taken from the plaza.

A section of the south side of Zuñi Pueblo, New Mexico.

A distant view of the Zuñi Pueblo.

A Zuñi girl with a water olla.

A group of Zuñi braves at their pueblo in New Mexico.

The war chief of the Zuñi Indians, taken in 1873.

The vegetable gardens surrounding the Zuñi Pueblo.

SANTA FE

A characteristic ruin of the Pueblo San Juan, New Mexico, on the north bank of the San Juan River, about fifteen miles west of the Canyon Largo.

The Church of San Miguel, the oldest in Sante Fe, New Mexico.

The altar of the Church of San Miguel. As O'Sullivan noted: "Many of the altar adornments are ancient and elaborate in the popular church style of two centuries ago."

One of the main streets of Sante Fe in 1874–75.

CANYON DE CHELLY

Head of Canyon de Chelly. Here, according to O'Sullivan the canyon walls "are 1200 feet in height."

Explorers' Column in the Canyon de Chelly. O'Sullivan gave its height as ninety feet with its base about seventy feet by one hundred.

O'Sullivan's famous photograph of the ruins in the Canyon de Chelly. The ruins are in a cavity in the rock wall, 60 feet above the present bed of the Canyon. The height of the walls here a about 700 feet. O'Sullivan took this picture in 1873.

An overall view of the Canyon de Chelly, now a National Park. A few of the expedition's tents are in the foreground.

7

THE LAST YEARS

He is an educated gentleman of superior qualifications in his profession and in every way personally worthy and a Tip Top Republican into the bargain.

Henry O'Connor, in his letter of recommendation for Tim O'Sullivan, 1880

Sometime in the fall or winter of 1875 Tim O'Sullivan returned to Staten Island. The simple dirt roads and clapboard farmhouses were a thousand years apart from the gay public square of Santa Fe, the awesome beauty of Canyon de Chelly, the hard-packed parade of Fort Whipple, the sinister silence of the Black Canyon, but it was home.

It was evident O'Sullivan now wanted roots. In December of that year he bought a small piece of land on Staten Island but curiously never built a house. It is still a vacant lot.[102] This is the last we hear of him for a few years.

When he returned to New York, O'Sullivan undoubtedly heard of Brady's financial difficulties. In 1872 the old photographer's New York business had collapsed in ruins when he was forced into Bankruptcy Court of the Southern District of New York. Bills for wages, chemicals, glass, clothing, rent, showered down on him. Finally the court declared Brady bankrupt in January 1873, when it was discovered the total business of Brady's New York and Washington galleries was less than $12,000 while the amount of indebtedness was over $25,000.

Under the court order Brady's goods were subject to seizure by the United States Marshal. But Brady conspired with the local Tammany-appointed sheriff, Matthew T. Brennan, and had nineteen cartloads of goods spirited from his New York gallery before the United States Marshal obtained an injunction.

Brady then fled to Washington, where he established legal residence. He was then about fifty years of age, wracked with rheumatism and barely able to see.

In Washington, Brady managed to save his gallery from his manager, A. Burgess—now headlining himself as "Successor to M. B. Brady"—by transferring title to his wife, then mortgaging his business to Mrs. Brady's brother, Samuel, her nephew, Levin C. Handy, and to a businessman of Washington, John Patch.[103]

Now Brady's goal was to get Congress to buy his wet-plate collection. In 1875 Congress finally provided, in the Appropriations Act, for a lump sum of $25,000 to be paid to Brady for a total of 5712 wet plates. Brady paid off his creditors and in July 1875 was released from bankruptcy.

The following year Brady received a stunning blow. He had prepared an expensive exhibit for the International Centennial Exhibition in Philadelphia, fully anticipating he would win first prize as he had done in the past. But all the awards went to the younger photographers, while he took a belated commendation for the value of his work as a historical record.

M. B. BRADY'S REGISTER,

No. of Negative.	NAME.	ADDRESS.
	August 25th 1873	
7416	L. H. L. Jordelle	
7417	Mrs Dr. Pope	
	August 26th 1873	
7418		
	August 27th 1873	
	M B Brady Closed in Bankr	
	Opened this day by Jno Pa...	October 4th 1873
7419	M Lansman	October 4 1873
	Oct. 7 1873.	
7420.	E. Tillitson	
7421	J. H. Williams ...	$5 was not paid till Oct 17.
7422	Mrs Townley	Oct. 9th
7423	Mr Geo R. Ludlam	Oct 9th
7424	Mrs Elizabeth Turner & Child	"

The end of an institution—Brady's Register with its notice of closing because of bankruptcy.

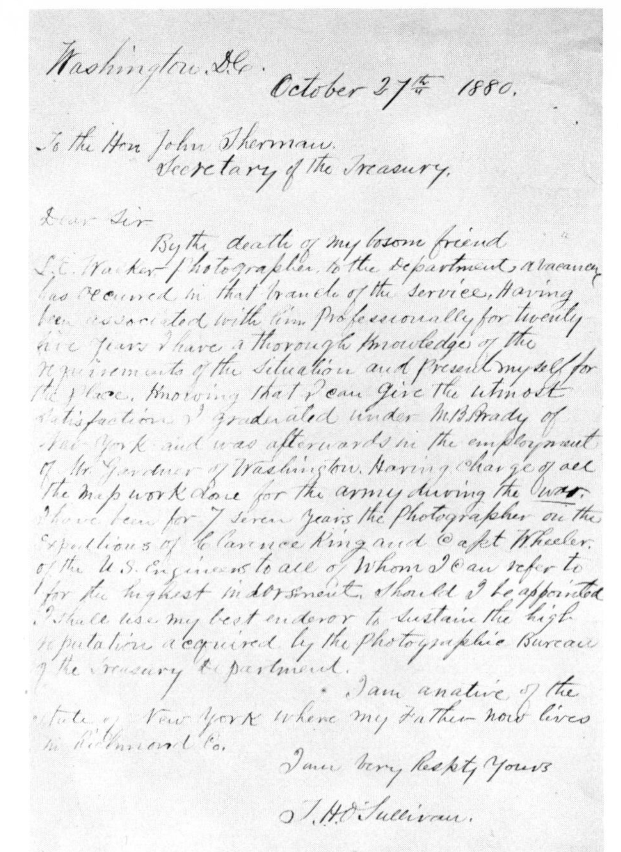

Washington D.C. October 27th 1880.

To the Hon John Sherman.
Secretary of the Treasury.

Dear Sir

By the death of my bosom friend L. E. Walker Photographer to the Department, a vacancy has occurred in that branch of the service. Having been associated with him professionally for twenty five years I have a thorough knowledge of the requirements of the situation and present myself for the place. Knowing that I can give the utmost satisfaction. I graduated under M.B.Brady of New York and was afterwards in the employment of Mr Gardner of Washington. Having charge of all the map work done for the army during the war. I have been for 7 seven years the Photographer on the Expeditions of Clarence King and Capt Wheeler of the U.S. Engineers to all of whom I can refer to for the highest indorsement. Should I be appointed I shall use my best endevor to sustain the high reputation acquired by the Photographic Bureau of the Treasury Department.

I am a native of the State of New York where my Father now lives in Richmond Co.

I am Very Respty Yours

T. H. O'Sullivan.

O'Sullivan's application for the position of "Chief Photographer."

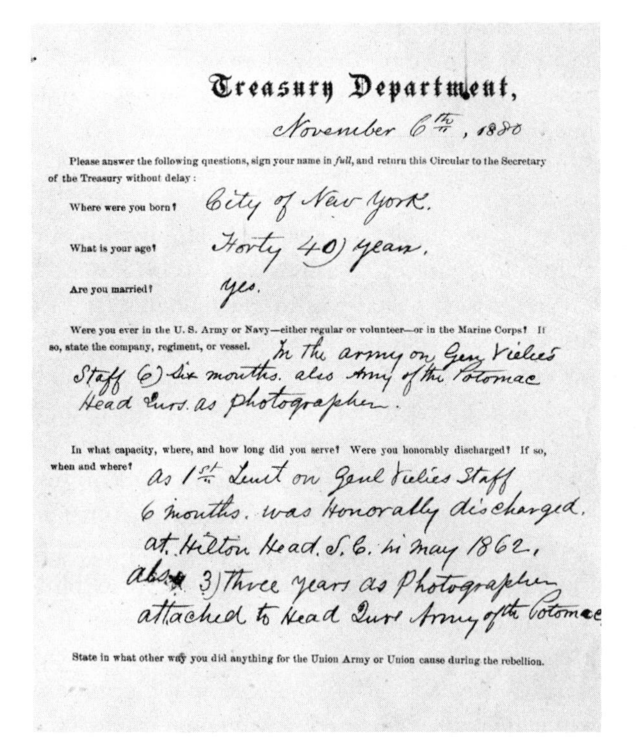

Treasury Department,

November 6th, 1880

Please answer the following questions, sign your name in *full*, and return this Circular to the Secretary of the Treasury without delay:

Where were you born? City of New York.

What is your age? Forty 40) years.

Are you married? yes.

Were you ever in the U. S. Army or Navy—either regular or volunteer—or in the Marine Corps? If so, state the company, regiment, or vessel. In the army on Genl Vielies Staff 6) six months. also Army of the Potomac Head Qurs. as photographer.

In what capacity, where, and how long did you serve? Were you honorably discharged? If so, when and where? as 1st Leut on Genl Vielies Staff 6 months. was Honorally discharged. at Hilton Head. S. C. in May 1862. also 3) Three years as Photographer attached to Head Qurs Army of the Potomac

State in what other way you did anything for the Union Army or Union cause during the rebellion.

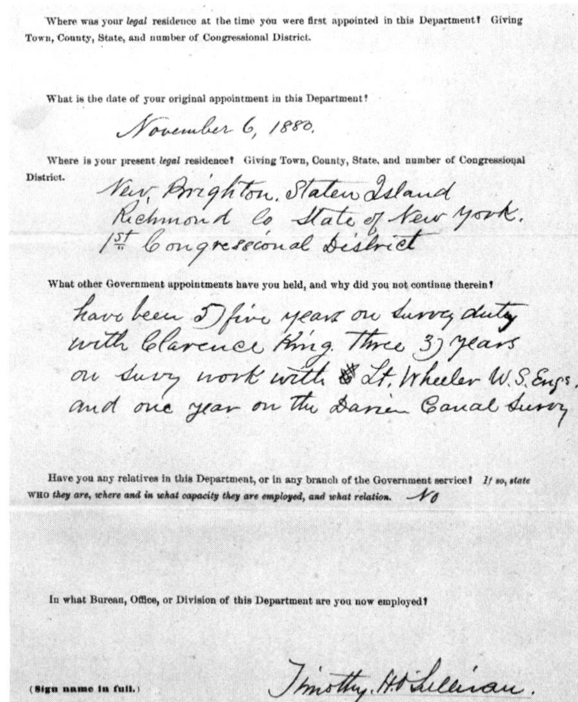

Where was your *legal* residence at the time you were first appointed in this Department? Giving Town, County, State, and number of Congressional District.

What is the date of your original appointment in this Department? November 6, 1880.

Where is your present *legal* residence? Giving Town, County, State, and number of Congressional District. New Brighton. Staten Island Richmond Co State of New York. 1st Congressional District

What other Government appointments have you held, and why did you not continue therein? have been 5) five years on survey duty with Clarence King. Three 3) years on survy work with Lt. Wheeler U. S. Engs. and one year on the Darien Canal Survey

Have you any relatives in this Department, or in any branch of the Government service? *If so, state* WHO *they are, where and in what capacity they are employed, and what relation.* No

In what Bureau, Office, or Division of this Department are you now employed?

(Sign name in full.) Timothy H. O'Sullivan.

The Treasury Department's questionnaire with O'Sullivan's answers and signature.

Photographers were now numerous in Washington. Among the most famous was Lewis E. Walker, attached to the Office of the Supervising Architect of the U. S. Treasury.

O'Sullivan was now the first photographer for the newly established United States Geological Survey, headed by his old Western commander, Clarence King, who had given him a temporary appointment at $100 a month.

O'Sullivan could not have been very active, however, for as Hermine M. Baumhofer points out in her study of O'Sullivan's records in the National Archives, the total photographic expenditures for the survey office in 1880 was only $6.75.

During these last five years O'Sullivan might have suffered some personal tragedy. We know he was now a widower and living with his father, Jeremiah, in New Brighton, Staten Island. Perhaps his wife had died suddenly and he had disposed of his home to live with his father, who apparently had always been close to him.[104]

Toward the end of 1880 Walker, whom O'Sullivan describes as "my bosom friend," died, leaving a vacancy as "chief photographer." The position carried a salary of $2250—handsome by the standards of 1880—and O'Sullivan was so anxious for the appointment he sought out recommendations from his close friends and former colleagues on the Western surveys.[105]

It only had to be known that Tim O'Sullivan needed recommendations and they came in by mail, messenger, and telegraph. George R. Finckel, Chief Clerk of the War Department, Clarence King, J. W. Powell, Alexander Gardner, Mathew Brady—they all rushed their recommendations to the Treasury Department.

Brady's letter—as usual someone else wrote it—stated he had known Tim "from boyhood and know that he is a thorough expert at his business and a very reliable man."

On the official stationery of the U. S. Engineer's Office—headed "Explorations West of the 100th Meridian," now the official name of his surveys—Wheeler, now a captain, wrote from Santa Fe that O'Sullivan was a fine photographer, a man of unquestionable integrity and executive ability.

Lieutenant Lull, who had commanded the U.S.S. *Guard* during the Selfridge Expedition was now a commander stationed in Washington and he rushed a letter over to the Treasury Department pointing out that despite the "climatic conditions" in the jungles of Darién, O'Sullivan's work was "outstanding."

"He was an especially desirable associate," Lull wrote, probably recalling those rough days aboard the *Guard*.

In November 1880 H. T. Crosby, Chief Clerk of the War Department, added his testimony about O'Sullivan's "worth and capacity."

There were many more officials in the United States Geological Survey, army, officers, scientists. All that fall letters and telegrams came into the office of the Secretary of the Treasury highly endorsing O'Sullivan as a photographer and praising him as an individual of courage and integrity.

Probably the most important one came on the morning of October 28 from Arizona. It wasn't a letter but a telegram from Clarence King, O'Sullivan's first chief on the Western surveys.

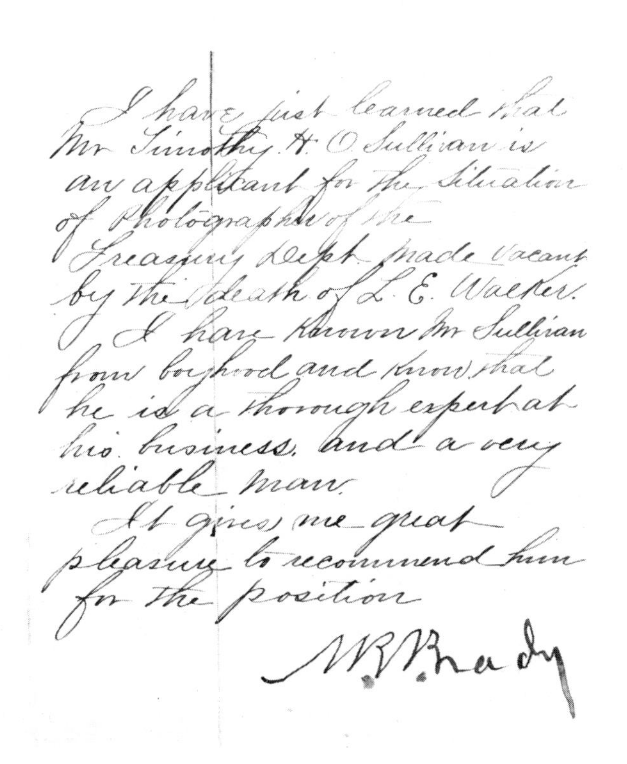
I have just learned that
Mr Timothy H. O Sullivan is
an applicant for the Situation
of Photographer of the
Treasury Dept made vacant
by the death of L. E. Walker.
I have known Mr Sullivan
from boyhood and know that
he is a thorough expert at
his business, and a very
reliable man.
It gives me great
pleasure to recommend him
for the position
M B Brady

Brady's letter of recommendation of O'Sullivan.

Blank No. 1. 262

THE WESTERN UNION TELEGRAPH COMPANY.

This Company TRANSMITS and DELIVERS messages only on conditions, limiting its liability, which have been assented to by the sender of the following message.
Errors can be guarded against only by repeating a message back to the sending station for comparison, and the Company will not hold itself liable for errors or delays in transmission or delivery of Unrepeated Messages.
This message is an UNREPEATED MESSAGE and is delivered by request of the sender, under the conditions named above.

A. R. BREWER, Sec'y. NORVIN GREEN, President.

Dated San Francisco Oct 28 1880

Received at

To T. H. O'Sullivan
Geological Survey
Wn DC

You are hereby authorized to present my compliments to the Hon Secretary of the Treasury & to say to him that I unqualifiedly recommend you for the Position of Photographer

READ THE NOTICE AT THE TOP.

Blank No. 1.

THE WESTERN UNION TELEGRAPH COMPANY.

This Company TRANSMITS and DELIVERS messages only on conditions, limiting its liability, which have been assented to by the sender of the following message.
Errors can be guarded against only by repeating a message back to the sending station for comparison, and the Company will not hold itself liable for errors or delays in transmission or delivery of Unrepeated Messages.
This message is an UNREPEATED MESSAGE and is delivered by request of the sender, under the conditions named above.

A. R. BREWER, Sec'y. NORVIN GREEN, President.

Dated Oct 28 1880

Received at

To 2 O.S

to the treasury From years of experience with you & your work I have no hesitancy in saying that you will not fail to give satisfaction in your technical work honesty & administration

READ THE NOTICE AT THE TOP.

Blank No. 1.

THE WESTERN UNION TELEGRAPH COMPANY.

This Company TRANSMITS and DELIVERS messages only on conditions, limiting its liability, which have been assented to by the sender of the following message.
Errors can be guarded against only by repeating a message back to the sending station for comparison, and the Company will not hold itself liable for errors or delays in transmission or delivery of Unrepeated Messages.
This message is an UNREPEATED MESSAGE and is delivered by request of the sender, under the conditions named above.

A. R. BREWER, Sec'y. NORVIN GREEN, President.

Dated Oct 28 1880

Received at

To 3 O.S

Capacity respectfully yours
Clarence King
Director

77 Paid Gk

new

READ THE NOTICE AT THE TOP.

Clarence King's three-page telegram recommending O'Sullivan for the post of "Chief Photographer."

Mathew Brady, a photograph in 1889 by L. C. Handy. He was sixty-eight at the time.

Like O'Sullivan, his teacher Mathew Brady was forgotten by most Americans in his last sad days. This is the house, torn down only a few years ago, where Brady spent his last days in Washington with his nieces. Pictured in the swing is one of his nieces, Alice Handy Cox, and Frederick Cox. Mrs. Cox spent a great deal of time with the author more than a decade ago when he was preparing his biography of Brady and told him family legends of O'Sullivan, some of which were later confirmed as fact. By L. C. Handy.

King, now a national figure, authorized O'Sullivan "to present my compliments to the Secretary of the Treasury that I unqualifiedly recommend you for the position of Photographer to the Treasurer. From years of experience with you and your work I have no hesitancy in saying that you will not fail in giving satisfaction in your technical work, honesty and administration."

The great J. W. Powell, now in charge of the Bureau of Ethnology, wrote a glowing letter to the Supervising Architect of the Treasury Department praising O'Sullivan's "great skill" with a camera.

On November 6, 1880, Tim O'Sullivan was appointed as official photographer for the U. S. Treasury Department and took the oath the same day.

By a bitter coincidence and almost to the day, the Brady National Photographic Art Gallery at 627 Pennsylvania Avenue, closed its doors forever. Brady and Julia had been reduced to living in the building occupied by the gallery, "finding the hotels and boarding houses were too expensive."[106]

Brady found employment with other photographers in Washington, sometimes in partnership, but it never seemed to work. The old master who had persuaded the Prince of Wales to come to his gallery in New York, who had posed Lincoln before his Cooper Union speech, who had cheerfully welcomed kings and queens, dictators, military heroes, and the great of the theater, who had gathered together an immortal collection of Civil War glass plates, was now, as someone said, "a sad, sick old man." Yet ironically he would outlive O'Sullivan by fourteen years.

On Staten Island, O'Sullivan, the man Brady had "known from boyhood" was dying in the second-floor bedroom of a clapboard house in West Brighton. Five months after he had taken the oath of office for his Treasury position,[107] Timothy O'Sullivan had resigned to return to his father's home.

Those bitter years with the Army of the Poto-

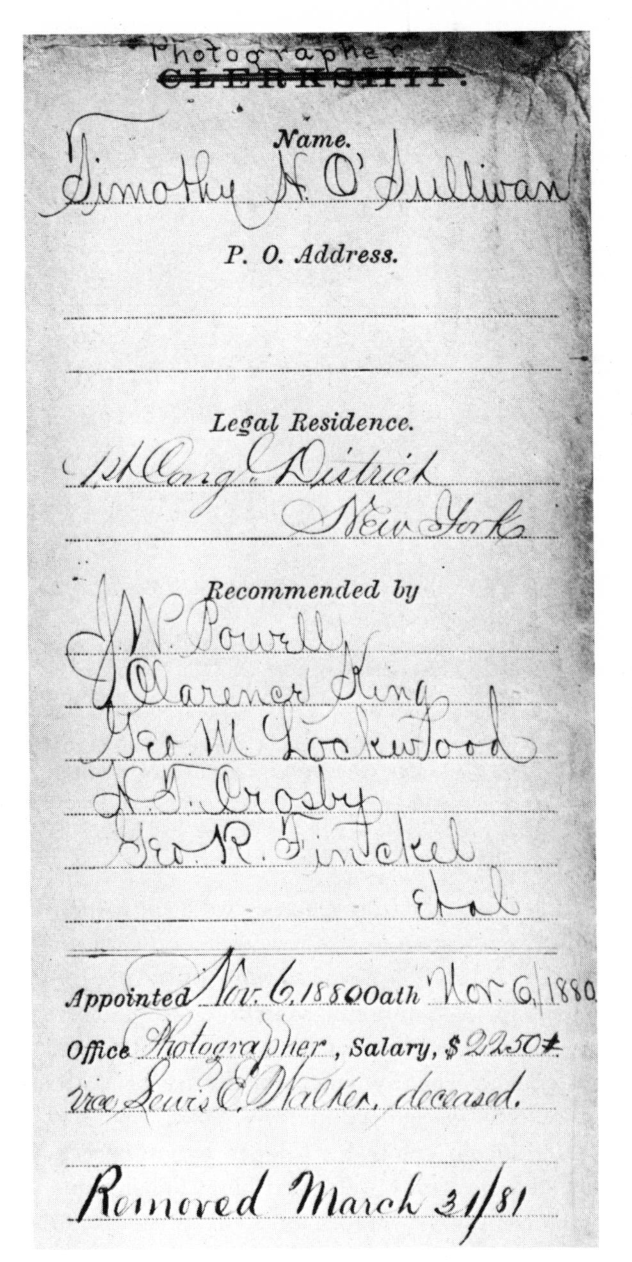

~~CLERKSHIP.~~ Photographer

Name.
Timothy H. O'Sullivan

P. O. Address.

Legal Residence.
1st Cong. District
New York

Recommended by
J. W. Powell
Clarence King
Geo. M. Lockwood
H. T. Crosby
Geo. R. Finckel
et al

Appointed Nov. 6, 1880 *Oath* Nov. 6, 1880
Office Photographer, *Salary, $* 2250
vice Louis E. Walker, deceased.

Removed March 31/81

The brief history of O'Sullivan's last employment —from Treasury Department files.

The memorial stone on Brady's grave.

St. Peter's Cemetery on Staten Island where O'Sullivan is buried in an unmarked grave.

mac, from Second Manassas to Appomattox, the numbing cold of the Western mountains and the blistering heat of the plains and the lonely deserts had at last caught up with the lanky O'Sullivan. He returned to Staten Island with an advanced case of tuberculosis.

Less than a year later, on the morning of January 14, 1882, with the first quiet snowflakes of a heavy storm beginning to whiten the roads and lanes and pastures of West Brighton, Tim O'Sullivan died at the age of forty-two.

The Indian nations O'Sullivan knew would soon be wiped out, the deep canyons and gorges lost in the waters of gigantic twentieth-century dams; cities would spring up out of the ramshackle log cabins and shacks he slept in and railroads would crisscross the wastelands where he had led his mules.

The deserts where he had almost died of thirst would quiver with the thunder of rockets, and the clean sharp air of Frenchman Flat, which he knew so well, would witness a ball of fire so huge, so terrifying that it would dwarf all the cannons he had ever known in his war had they been placed wheel to wheel from Gettysburg to Fort Fisher.

For future generations of Americans, the Great West would not be the same. Only through the eyes of Tim O'Sullivan's camera would they know it as it was.

FOOTNOTES

1. O'Sullivan was first credited with taking the Gettysburg pictures by Alexander Gardner in his two-volume *Sketch Book of the Civil War* (hereafter cited as *Sketch Book*), published by Philip & Solomon, Washington, D.C., 1865, and a set of stereos, also published by Philip & Solomon, Washington, D.C., 1866. Eighty of the stereos with many rare views are in the New York Historical Society. Prints of his photographs are also in the Brady Collection, Library of Congress.

2. *Harper's Weekly,* July 22, 1863, devoted most of its issue to the Gettysburg photographs and on page two had this small piece, crediting Brady with the photographs. There was no mention of O'Sullivan, although in the August 22 issue there was another four-column woodcut credited to Alexander Gardner.

3. O'Sullivan's death certificate was located in the Idle Records Department, Bureau of Vital Statistics, Board of Health, Albany, New York. The microfilm is very faint and the words are barely discernible.

However, under a powerful glass we find O'Sullivan was listed as forty-two years old, widowed, occupation photographer, birthplace Ireland, father's name Jeremiah, mother's name, Ann D. He died in West Brighton, Staten Island of tuberculosis, January 14, 1882, and was buried in St. Peter's, New Brighton. Ironically his name is listed as "Sullivan" an error which occurs in other vital statistical listing. In some documents his name is listed both ways. A search of the files of all the weekly newspapers on Staten Island failed to turn up an obit for O'Sullivan. However, it was the custom of the day not to use an obituary unless relatives personally delivered it to the newspaper office. The Philadelphia *Photographic Magazine* did have four lines, stating O'Sullivan "died at the home of a relative." He died at his father's home in West Brighton, Staten Island.

4. In 1869 *Harper's New Monthly* published an article "Photographs from the High Rockies" by John Sampson. Curiously, although the article is about O'Sullivan he is not mentioned by name. Sampson points out that the photographer had several narrow escapes during the Civil War. There is little doubt that O'Sullivan saw a great deal of the war and was under fire many times. We know he was at Petersburg when the Union and Confederate artillery were trading shells, and Gardner's *Sketch Book,* the stereos published by Philip & Solomon, and his plates in the Brady-Handy Collection, Library of Congress, show he was on many battlefields. Out of the hundred prints in Gardner's two volumes, forty-five were made from O'Sullivan's negatives.

5. The lithographic illustrations in the Selfridge Report are chiefly copies of the O'Sullivan photographs although John Moran was the photographer on the 1871 Selfridge Survey and a few of his photographs are included. John Moran was the brother of the American artist Thomas Moran. Both were members of a famous family of artists.

6. O'Sullivan is buried in St. Peter's Cemetery, Staten Island, according to his death certificate. Mr. James Fitzgerald reports, however, that a search of the existing records and the tombstones in the ancient cemetery failed to disclose his grave.

7. The exhibition took place at Chilton's, the chemist shop owned by James R. Chilton, 263 Broadway, as reported in the *Journal of Commerce,* September 28, 1839.

8. See *Mathew Brady: Historian With a Camera* by James D. Horan, p. 88. (Hereafter cited as Horan.)

9. *The Daguerreotype in America* by Beaumont Newhall. New York: Duell, Sloan & Pearce, 1961, p. 57. (Hereafter cited as Newhall.)

In 1955, in my biography of Brady, I tried to establish whether illiteracy or poor eyesight was the cause for the lack of Brady letters. I concluded it was impossible to tell from the lack of evidence. However, since then, Beaumont Newhall, Curator of the Eastman House in Rochester and an imminent photographic historian, has uncovered this new Brady letter, which would seem to indicate that Brady was not illiterate. We have had a few Brady signatures on official papers (bankruptcy, bill of sale for his New York City property) but this new find and the letter he wrote to Morse in 1855 are apparently the only available thus far. Several years ago a collection of Brady's plates turned up in an old upstate New York barn. We are always hoping some of his letters—and now O'Sullivan's—might be found in the same fashion.

10. *Photographic Art Journal,* vol. I, 1851, p. 136, and Horan, p. 18, and the undated clipping which Brady's nieces allowed me to copy in 1954.

11. Letter in the J. Pierpont Morgan Library, New York City, and first published in *The Daguerreotype in America,* by Beaumont Newhall, p. 82.

12. Robert Taft, *Photography and the American Scene.* New York: The Macmillan Company, 1938, p. 59. (Hereafter cited as Taft.)

13. Circuit Court, District of Columbia, 1848–1858, Chancery Book, no. r, Case 613, Brady vs Heyden (Record Group 21, in the National Archives).

14. *National Intelligencer,* June 21, 1858.

15. *Mathew B. Brady's Photographic Gallery in Washington* by Josephine Cobb, Records of the Columbia Historical Society of Washington, D.C., vols. 53–56. (Washington, 1959), p. 41–44. (Hereafter cited as Cobb.)

16. An excellent article on Brady on Staten Island by Roswell S. Coles appeared in the Staten Island *Historian,* April–June 1946. I have found a few references to Brady's Staten Island residence, such as Morris' *History of Staten Island,* published in 1898, vol. 2, p. 237, which has Brady entertaining "distinguished guests." Dr. Vernon Hampton's *Staten Island's Claim to Fame,* published in 1924, p. 124, has Brady receiving his "distinguished guests from various parts of America at his residence on Grymes Hill, Staten Island . . ."

Documentation for William Page's residence on the Island can be found in "Staten Island Artists" by Dorothy Smith in the *Historian* for July 1939, (vol. II, no. 3). Miss Smith reveals Page returned to Staten Island to reside at the famous "Octagon House" in Tottenville in 1860 until his death in 1885.

Dr. Hampton claims in his book that Brady was conducting "experiments" in photography in 1839 when Draper was known to have lived on Staten Island. Dr. Hampton gives no documentation for this and I find it hard to believe. I agree with his assumption that Brady worked with both Page and Draper in the early years before he established his Fulton Street Gallery.

There is another little-known historical item which is admittedly tenuous but still a link in the Brady-to-O'Sullivan-to-Staten Island. Dr. Samuel McKenzie Elliott, the New York City oculist, moved to Staten Island about 1835 and built a house on Grymes Hill called "The Tower House." Elliott was a great promoter of building developments in West Brighton, where O'Sullivan lived. We know from the trade journals Brady was bothered with weak eyes. Is it not reasonable to link Brady with Dr. Elliott, the New York oculist, who would bring Brady to Staten Island and thus tie him in with O'Sullivan?

17. In 1954 Mrs. Cox told me the story of O'Sullivan simply as an accepted family legend. Brady in 1880 did recall in his letter of recommendation that he had known O'Sullivan "since boyhood"—undoubtedly on Staten Island.

18. Newhall, p. 110.

19. George Alfred "Gath" Townsend's interview with Brady in the New York *World,* April 12, 1891, p. 23. (Hereafter cited as Townsend.)

20. Legend has Allan Pinkerton also writing a pass for Brady but I have examined the Pinkerton Archives since the late 1940s and I have been unable to find a letter to Brady or any about Brady. Ironically there is a letter from Allan Pinkerton praising Alexander Gardner as one of the best of the Civil War photographers.

21. Alexander Gardner's letter, March 23, 1861, mentions that "carte-de-visite negatives of nearly all my gallery" were being sent to Anthony "for publication." See correspondence of Captain Montgomery C. Meigs, records, of the office of the Architect of the Capitol.

22. "Photographs from the High Rockies" by John Sampson, *Harper's New Monthly Magazine,* September 1869. (Hereafter cited as Sampson.)

23. Cobb, p. 52.

24. Miss Josephine Cobb of the National Archives is known to every historian who has delved in the iconography of the Civil War. Her invaluable "Photographers of the Civil War" published in *Military Affairs,* vol. XXVI, no. 3, Fall 1962, is the result of her extensive work on the subject. Her article contains a list of Civil War photographers and their assistants with military units. Gardner is listed as attached to the Headquarters, Army of the Potomac at Brandy Station, "for taking views on the march," along with O'Sullivan, Samuel Ott, John Reekie, S. F. Denny, James Gardner, and as being associated with Mark Cohen.

For eyewitness accounts of Civil War photographers see *Anthony's Photographic Bulletin,* no. 2, and the *Photographic History of the Civil War* (ten volumes), Francis Trevelyan Miller, Editor-in-Chief, Review of Reviews Co., 1912, N.Y. (Hereafter cited as Miller's.)

25. "Photographers of the Civil War" by Josephine Cobb, *Military Affairs,* vol. XXVI, no. 3, Fall 1962, p. 128–129.

26. "The Confederate Gunners," p. 258, Miller's, vol. V, *Forts and Artillery.*

27. The Elk Mountain pictures have been credited to Alexander Gardner but a stereo published by Philip & Solomon in 1863 has the prints developed by Gardner from a negative by O'Sullivan. O'Sullivan is also credited with this photo in the Library of Congress Brady-Handy Collection.

28. *Harper's Weekly,* August 27, 1863. Woodcuts of course were used, the scenes based on O'Sullivan's pictures. Newspaper reproductions did not come until many years later.

29. In my opinion this set of photographs are as good as anything taken in World War II. One gets the feeling of restless Grant, moving from general to general, collecting every opinion which he must evaluate, and then eventually making his decision. The series also demonstrates O'Sullivan's dramatic sense. How static the pictures would have been, taken on ground level.

30. *Clarence King: Memoirs.* Published for the King Memorial Committee of the Century Association by G. P. Putnam's Sons, New York and London, 1904. This volume consists of more than twelve articles written by close friends of King and some members of the King Expedition. (Hereafter cited as King.)

31. "The King Survey," *North American Review,* vol. CXIII, July 1871.

32. In addition to scientific reports prepared by the surveys (King, eight; Wheeler, forty), volumes of O'Sullivan's photographs were included. They are extremely rare today. The King set which I own is practically unobtainable outside of the National Archives and the Library of Congress.

33. *The Year of Decision: 1846,* by B. De Voto, p. 359.

34. *Great Surveys of the American West,* by Richard A. Bartlett. Norman, Oklahoma: University of Oklahoma Press, 1962, p. 123. One of the best-written books on the Western surveys. (Hereafter cited as Bartlett.)

35. King, p. 187.

36. King. p. 160.

37. King's book on mountaineering is still read. He had a vivid, descriptive prose, for example, his view from Mount Whitney:

"The day was cloudless and sky, milder than is common over these extreme heights, warmed to a mellow glow and rested in softening beauty over minaret and dome. Air and light seemed melted together even the wild rocks springing up all about us wore an aspect of aerial delicacy. Around the wild panorama, half low desert, half rugged granite mountains, each detail was observable, a uniform luminous medium toned with obscuring the field of vision . . . now it was like an opal world, submerged in a sea of dreamy light, down through whose motionless, transparent depths I became conscious of indescribable depths, reefs of pearly granite, as clear and delicate as the coral banks in a tropical sea . . ."

38. "Clarence King, Geologist" by Samuel Franklin Emmons, *American Journal of Science,* March 1902.

39. King, p. 330–332.

40. Robert Ridgway in *The Condor,* vol. XXX, no. 1, January–February 1928. (Hereafter cited as Ridgway.)

41. King, p. 385.

42. John Sampson's "Photographs from the High Rockies," *Harper's New Monthly Magazine,* vol. XXXIX, September 1869. (Hereafter cited as Sampson.) This is a strange article. Since I cited it in my book on Brady in 1955 I have been trying to learn something about the author, "Sampson," but without success. For some reason he does not name O'Sullivan but talks of him only as "the photographer." Unquestionably the photographer was O'Sullivan. The woodcuts accompanying the article are definitely based on his photographs. Bartlett raises the question whether "Sampson" might be O'Sullivan. I doubt it. O'Sullivan might have hesitated to allow the use of his name in the Sampson article for a number of reasons, clearance by King, contract, government regulations, etc.

43. Mark Twain's *Roughing It,* p. 151.

44. Sampson, p. 469.

45. Sampson, p. 469–70.

46. Sampson, p. 467, and Ridgway, p. 24.

47. Sampson, p. 467–68, and *Nevada: a Guide to the Silver State,* p. 143.

48. Sampson, p. 468.

49. Sampson, p. 471, and Ridgway, p. 24–25.

50. Ridgway, p. 24–25. The ambulance Ridgway refers to is the Civil War type O'Sullivan used as a traveling darkroom, similar to the one he used in the Civil War. O'Sullivan later photographed it in the desert.

51. Sampson, p. 472–73.

52. "Ornithology," *Report of the Geological Exploration of the Fortieth Parallel,* vol. IV, part III, p. 353. Also Ridgway, p. 25.

53. Bartlett, p. 168.

54. Bartlett, p. 172, quoting from *Copy Book of Letters,* July 10, 1868, August 13, 1868, February 14, 1871.

55. Sampson, p. 471.

56. Sampson, p. 472.

57. Sampson, p. 473.

58. WPA State Guide Series, *Nevada,* p. 163–164.

59. "Ornithology," *Report of the Geological Exploration of the Fortieth Parallel,* vol. I, part III, p. 358.

60. Sampson, p. 472.

61. I believe this is another instance of O'Sullivan's fine work. Here he repeated his technique of Bethseda, where he took Grant and his generals from the church steeple; instead of a static picture of a wagon and mule team he placed them in the proper dramatic perspective.

62. Sampson, p. 472.

63. Bartlett, p. 175.

64. New York *World,* January 21, 1870.

65. *Mathew Brady: Historian With a Camera.* See also Cobb p. 57–62.

66. Cobb, p. 54.

67. Brady was still in Washington that year and Gardner had returned from Kansas. The only authenticated photograph we have of O'Sullivan is the one he took in 1870 in Darién (see page x). There is a Civil War photograph of O'Sullivan, tentatively identified. It shows a slender, lanky man with a bearded, weather-beaten face.

68. Bartlett, p. 177.

69. *Correspondence of the Darién Expedition,* p. 6. This is a 256-page log of the official correspondence of the expedition, written probably by a noncommissioned officer. Most of the correspondence consists of Selfridge's official letters and the paymaster's lists. (Owned by the author. Hereafter cited as Log.)

70. Log, p. 226. Also see the log of the *Guard.* (Hereafter cited as the *Guard.*)

71. Log of the U.S.S. *Guard.* A two-hundred-page journal of the day-to-day events aboard the storeship.

72. Log, p. 37.

73. Log, p. 39.

74. Log, p. 67.

75. Despite the difficulties of weather and the thick jungle, O'Sullivan took a number of excellent photographs.

76. Log, p. 62.

77. Log, p. 69.

78. Log, p. 70.

79. Log, p. 107–116.

80. New York *Times,* December 7, 1875, p. 2. At the time there were 169 posts, 130 west of the Mississippi. The largest was Fort Sill, Indian Territory, with 550 men. Many of the forts O'Sullivan visited were mere cabins, as his pictures show; Fort Defiance, Fort Whipple, etc., with few men and officers and weary wives.

81. Captain George M. Wheeler, "Geographical Report," in *Report upon United States Geographical Surveys West of the One Hundredth Meridian,* 30, p. 34–35. (Hereafter cited as Wheeler.)

82. Frederick W. Loring, "A Council of War," *Appleton's Journal of Literature, Science and Art,* volume VI, no. 124, August 12, 1871, p. 182–183. (Hereafter cited as Loring.)

83. Loring, p. 182.

84. Loring, p. 183.

85. Wheeler, "Geographical Report," p. 45.

86. Undated clipping, Bancroft Library, Berkeley, California. Wheeler Scrapbook, P.W. 32, vol. I. (Hereafter cited as Scrapbook.)

87. Undated clipping, Scrapbook.

88. Undated clipping, apparently the Inyo *Independent* from Major Egbert's later letter to the newspaper answering the charges.

89. Undated clipping, apparently the *Independent.*

90. Clipping, undated, not identified, picking up an article from the Inyo *Independent.*

91. Letter by Major Egbert to the editor of *The Independence* (Scrapbook). Egbert must have meant the Inyo *Independent.*

92. Undated and unidentified clipping in Scrapbook.

93. Wheeler, "Geographical Report, " p. 35.

94. Wheeler, "Geographical Report," pp. 169–170.

95. The picture, a stereo, shows the four boats, the dock, and the Indians.

96. Extracts from Notebooks no. 4 and 5 of G. K. Gilbert, relating to the Wheeler boat trip upstream on the Colorado River from Virgin River to Diamond Creek, hereafter cited as Gilbert.

97. Gilbert, p. 3.

98. O'Sullivan took Loring's picture two days before he was killed. It shows a grinning, cocky young man in a high-crowned hat leaning against his mule, Evil Merodach.

99. The Mohave's name was Maiman, a guide and interpreter for Wheeler who liked Loring.

100. Bartlett, p. 353–356.

101. Wheeler letters, Wheeler Collection, National Archives.

102. The deed to the land O'Sullivan purchased in 1875 and the deed to the house purchased by his father were discovered in the County Clerk's Office, St. George, Staten Island. Jeremiah O'Sullivan's deed is Liber 31 of Deeds; Timothy O'Sullivan's, III of Deeds.

103. Cobb, p. 64–65.

104. There is a complete absence of facts on O'Sullivan for these years. I tried to locate his wife's death certificate and their marriage certificate without success.

105. Letters recommending Timothy H. O'Sullivan as Chief Photographer, Treasury Department, Treasury Department files. National Archives. (Hereafter cited as Recommendations.)

106. There is a poignant last entry in Brady's Washington Register: "Mathew Brady Closed by Bankruptcy." See also Cobb, p. 67. Brady died in the "alms ward," Presbyterian Hospital, January 15, 1896, alone and forgotten.

107. Recommendations. The formal oath is signed by O'Sullivan giving his address as Staten Island. A signed letter states he was living with his father.

BIBLIOGRAPHY

UNPUBLISHED GOVERNMENT DOCUMENTS (NATIONAL ARCHIVES)

THE WHEELER SURVEY:

Record Group 77—Records of the Office of the Chief of Engineers. This includes orders, commands, lists of personnel, and some of Wheeler's correspondence. There are minor letters from Wheeler to O'Sullivan.

THE KING SURVEY:

Record Group 57—This includes King's "Copy Book" of letters sent to General Humphreys from 1867 to 1879.

Logbook of the U.S.S. *Guard,* storeship of the Darién Expedition, December 1869–December 1870. The logbook of the *Guard,* to which O'Sullivan was attached, briefly mentions him. By a strange coincidence one scientist was named Sullivan. O'Sullivan is usually referred to as "the photographer."

THE SELFRIDGE EXPEDITION: (Owned by the author)

Correspondence of the Darién Expedition. This large logbook contains the official correspondence of Lieutenant Commander Thomas O. Selfridge to Secretary of the Navy George M. Robeson, along with commands, orders, lists of personnel, letters to Panama officials, etc., from December 31, 1869 to December 20, 1870. O'Sullivan is mentioned briefly as "the photographer" and is listed on the payroll and on the wardroom list of the U.S.S. *Guard.* Also included is the amount of photographic supplies he purchased from Anthony and Son in New York City before the *Guard* left from the Brooklyn Navy Yard for Darién.

PUBLISHED GOVERNMENT DOCUMENTS

(The King Reports are illustrated by engravings adapted from O'Sullivan's photographs. Wheeler's reports contain special volumes of O'Sullivan photographs.)

Catalogue and Index of the Hayden, King, and Wheeler Surveys, U. S. Geological Survey, Bulletin No. 222, Washington, 1904.

King, Clarence, *First Annual Report of the United States Geological Survey, to the Hon. Carl Schurz, Secretary of the Interior,* 1880.

———, *Professional Papers of the Engineers Department, U. S. Army,* 7 vols.

Wheeler, Captain George M., *Preliminary Report of Explorations on Nevada and Arizona,* 42 Cong., 2 Sess., Sen. Exec. Doc. 65, Washington, 1872.

———, *Report upon the United States Geological Survey West of the One Hundredth Meridian,* 7 vols., Washington, 1875–1889.

OFFICIAL RECORDS

O'Sullivan's Death Certificate, Idle Records, Department of Health, Bureau of Vital Statistics, Albany, New York.

Record of Jeremiah O'Sullivan land purchase, July 22, 1853, Liber 31 of Deeds, County Clerk's Office, St. George, Staten Island.

Record of Timothy H. O'Sullivan's purchase of land, Liber III of Deeds, County Clerk's Office, St. George, Staten Island.

O'Sullivan's letter asking for the position as chief photographer for the U. S. Treasury Department and the letters of recommendation, U. S. Treasury files, National Archives.

O'Sullivan's military pass, allowing him to enter Union lines as a photographer. Commands, Army of the Potomac (Record Group 98), vols. 78 (211A) and 83 (211 and 212) National Archives.

Captain Wheeler's Scrapbook, The Bancroft Library, University of California.

BOOKS

Adams, Henry. *The Education of Henry Adams.* New York, 1931.

Dellenbaugh, Frederick S. *A Canyon Voyage.* New York, 1908.

————*The Romance of the Colorado River.* New York, 1902.

De Voto, Bernard. *The Year of Decision: 1848.* Boston, 1943.

Doggett's New York City Directories, 1850–1861.

Donald, David H., ed. *Divided We Fought: a Pictorial History of the Civil War, 1861–1865.* By Hirst Milhollen, Milton Kaplan, and others. New York, 1952.

Driggs, Harold R., and William H. Jackson. *The Pioneer Photographer.* New York, 1929.

Ford, Worthington Chauncey, ed. *Letters of Henry Adams (1858–1891).* Boston, 1930.

Freeman, Louis. *The Colorado River: Yesterday, Today and Tomorrow.* New York, 1923.

Goetzmann, William H. *Army Exploration in the American West.* New Haven, Connecticut, 1960. (This is another excellent study of earlier army explorations in the West 1803–1863.)

Horan, James D. *Mathew Brady: Historian With a Camera.*

Jackson, William Henry, *Time Exposure,* New York, 1940.

King, Clarence. *Mountaineering in the Sierra Nevada.* Boston, 1872.

Meredith, Roy. *Mr. Lincoln's Cameraman.* New York, 1951.

Milhollen, Hirst, and Donald H. Mugridge. *Civil War Photographs.* Washington, 1961.

Miller, Francis Trevelyan, ed. *Photographic History of the Civil War* (in ten volumes). New York, Review of Reviews Corp., 1912.

Morgan, Dale L. *The Great Salt Lake.* New York, 1947.

Newhall, Beaumont. *The Daguerreotype in America,* New York, 1961.

Newhall, Beaumont and Nancy. *Master of Photography.* New York, 1958.

Pollack, Peter. *The Picture History of Photography.* New York, 1958.

Root, Marcus A. *The Camera and the Pencil.* New York, 1864.

Sachse, Julius F. "Early Daguerreotype Days" in *American Journal of Photography,* XIII (1892) 241–49, 305–15, 355–62, 403–10, 451–59, 543–50; XIV (1893) 369–77; XVI (1895) 359–66, 306–10; XVII (1896) 552–57.

Shearer, F. E., ed. *The Pacific Tourist: an Illustrated Guide to the Pacific Railroad and California, and Pleasure Resorts Across the Continent.* New York, Adams and Bishop Publishers, Copyright 1879 by Henry T. Williams, 1885 edition, p. 186–197. (Fertile source of information about the West, including descriptions of most towns and scenic attractions, local color, and short articles. Clarence King contributed an article, "The Great Shoshone Falls," describing his 1868 trip. Moran engravings of Shoshone Falls, p. 186 and 189, are adaptations from O'Sullivan photos, and others in this volume may be also.)

Taft, Robert. *Photography and the American Scene.* New York, 1938.

ARTICLES

Adams, Henry. Editorial Comments on the King Expedition Survey, *North American Review,* vol. CXIII, no. 233 (July 1871), 204.

Baumhofer, Hermine M. "T. H. O'Sullivan," Image, *Journal of Photography of the George Eastman House,* April 1953.

Cobb, Josephine. "Alexander Gardner," Image, 1958.

————. "Photographers of the Civil War," *Military Affairs,* vol. XXVI, no. 3, Fall 1962.

————. "Mathew B. Brady's Photographic Gallery in Washington," records of the Columbia Historical Society of Washington, D.C., vols. 53–56 (Washington, 1959) p. 28–69.

Coles, Roswell S. "Mathew B. Brady," *The Staten Island Historian.* April–June, 1946.

Darrah, William Culp, ed. "The Colorado Expedition of 1869" in *Utah Historical Quarterly,* vol. XV (1947).

————. "Frederick Samuel Dellenbaugh" in *Utah Historical Quarterly,* vols. XVI–XVII (1948–1949).

Dickason, David H. "Henry Adams and Clarence King, the Record of a Friendship" in *New England Quarterly,* vol. XVII, no. 2, June 1944.

Emmons, Samuel Franklin. "Biographical Memoir of Clarence King" in National Academy of Science, Biographical Memoirs, vol. VI (1909).

Fingado, Raymond C. "Photography on Staten Island" in *The Staten Island Historian,* January 1940.

Flato, Charles. "M. B. Brady and his Photos" in *Hound and Horn,* vol. VII, 1933.

Harris, Harry. "Robert Ridgway" in *The Condor,* vol. XXX, no. 1. January–February 1928.

Loring, Frederick W. "A Council of War" in *Appleton's Journal of Literature, Science and Art,* vol. VI, no. 124 (August 12, 1871).

————. "A Glimpse of Mormonism" in *Appleton's Journal of Literature, Science and Art,* vol. VI, no. 125 (August 19, 1871).

————. "Into the Valley of Death" in *Appleton's Journal of Literature, Science and Art,* vol. VI, no. 138 (November 18, 1871).

Newhall, Beaumont, "Landmark Camera, Research by Warren C. Stevens," *Photography,* December 1964.

————. Early Western Photographers, *Arizona Highways,* May 1946.

————. "Photography in the Civil War," in Museum of Modern Art, New York, 1937.

Sampson, John. "Photographs from the High Rockies" in *Harper's New Monthly Magazine,* vol. XXXIX, no. 232 (September 1869).

Smith, Henry Nash. "Clarence King, John Wesley Powell and the Establishment of the United States Geological Survey" in *Mississippi Valley Historical Review,* vol. XXXIV, no. 1, 1947.

INDEX OF TIMOTHY O'SULLIVAN PHOTOGRAPHS

INDEX